Information Systems Engineering Library

Testing Criteria for the SSADM Version 4 Tools Conformance Scheme

CCTA
August 1993
London: HMSO

Testing Criteria for the SSADM
Version 4 Tools Conformance Scheme

The questionnaire contained in this volume may be freely reproduced for the purpose of testing software. Completed questionnaires may not be used for advertising without the prior consent of CCTA and the permission of the author of the completed form. The text is crown copyright and may <u>not</u> be reproduced without the permission of the Controller of HMSO.

© Crown Copyright 1993

Applications for reproduction should be made to HMSO

First published 1993

ISBN 0 11 330590 7

ISSN 0967 9561

For further information regarding this publication and other CCTA products please contact:

    Riverwalk House
    157-161 Millbank
    London SW1P 4RT

    071-217-3331

Foreword

The **Information Systems Engineering Library** provides guidance on carrying out Information Systems Engineering activities. In the IS life cycle, Information Systems Engineering takes place once the IS strategy has been defined. It is concerned with the development of information systems up to the operational stage, when an information system becomes the responsibility of infrastructure management.

The Information Systems Engineering Library builds on the guidance in the CCTA IS Guides B set: *Systems Development Set* and complements other CCTA products, in particular the IS project management method, PRINCE, and the systems analysis and design method, SSADM.

The Information Systems Engineering Library is of interest to IS providers, helping them to improve the quality and productivity of their IS development work. It is also of interest to business managers, whose business operations depend on having effective IS support by means of Information Systems Engineering activities.

CCTA welcomes customer views on Information Systems Engineering Library publications. Please send your comments to:

> Customer Services
> Information Systems Engineering Group
> Gildengate House
> Upper Green Lane
> Norwich NR3 1DW

Testing Criteria for the SSADM
Version 4 Tools Conformance Scheme

Acknowledgements

The assistance of Warren Wright under contract to CCTA from the SSADM Research Centre at the University of Central England in Birmingham is gratefully acknowledged.

Testing Criteria for the SSADM
Version 4 Tools Conformance Scheme

Contents

Foreword		i
Acknowledgements		iii
Part A	Introduction and guidance on using the testing criteria	1
1	Introduction	3
2	The testing criteria questionnaire	5
3	Use of the questionnaire in appraisals	13
4	Presentation of results summaries and conformance certificate	19
Part B	Testing criteria	25
5	Business system options	27
6	Data flow modelling	41
7	Dialogue design	87
8	Entity event modelling	129
9	Function definition	165
10	Logical data modelling	195
11	Logical database process design	227
12	Processing specification	245
13	Relational data analysis	253
14	Requirements definition	263
15	Specification prototyping	279
16	Technical system options	291
17	Physical data design	299
18	Physical process specification	305
19	Physical environment description	311
20	Miscellaneous	327
Annex A	Index of products and concepts	329
Bibliography		335

Part A:

Introduction and guidance on using the testing criteria.

Testing Criteria for the SSADM
Version 4 Tools Conformance Scheme

1 Introduction

1.1 Purpose

The SSADM Version 4 Tools Conformance Scheme ('the scheme') provides a means by which potential customers of CASE tools may know the extent to which any CASE tool delivers products which conform to BS[nnnn]: *Specification for information systems products using SSADM* ('the British Standard').

The scheme has two supporting CCTA documents:

- this volume,

  and

- the Information Systems Engineering (ISE) Library volume *A Guide to the SSADM Version 4 Tools Conformance Scheme*.

The purpose of this volume is to provide independent testing organisations (approved by the SSADM Design Authority Board) with the detailed information they require to appraise CASE tools for conformance to SSADM Version 4.

It also shows how independent testing organisations are to present summaries of the results of testing and the contents of a conformance certificate. Such summaries will enable potential purchasers and evaluators of SSADM tools to compare the strengths and weaknesses of SSADM support provided by different tools.

This volume also enables suppliers or potential purchasers of CASE tools to conduct their own appraisals of tools if they wish to do so.

Testing Criteria for the SSADM
Version 4 Tools Conformance Scheme

1.2 Who should read this volume

This volume is directed at the following audience:

- purchasers and evaluators of CASE tools to support SSADM Version 4
- independent conformance testing organisations (and individual consultants who offer independent conformance testing)
- suppliers and builders of Version 4 software tools.

1.3 Structure of the volume

Chapter 2 describes how the testing criteria are set out.

Chapter 3 gives guidance on interpreting and using the criteria in appraisals.

Chapter 4 describes how independent testing organisations are to present summaries of appraisal results, so that fair comparisons can be made between tools.

Chapter 5 onwards contains the testing criteria for measuring a tool's conformance to SSADM Version 4. The criteria are set out as a questionnaire to help the tester tally results and calculate conformance percentages. The questionnaire is arranged in chapters, one for each product grouping. Within each chapter tests are given for

- all the *products* in the grouping
- the *concepts* found within those products.

A list of products and concepts covered is given at the start of each chapter.

Annex A contains an index to the products and concepts tested in the scheme, with references to entity identifiers used in the tests and cross-references to the chapters of the SSADM Version 4 Reference Manual where the technique which creates the product or concept is described.

2 The Testing Criteria Questionnaire

2.1 Derivation of testing criteria

In the scheme, 'conformance' means a measure of the extent to which CASE tools assist practitioners of SSADM create products that conform to the British Standard.

Conformance assessment is made against a list of testing criteria that have been derived directly from the British Standard's product specifications. This volume contains the testing criteria, arranged into an easy-to-use questionnaire which facilitates the testing process.

2.2 Structure of the questionnaire

A diagram illustrating the structure of the questionnaire is provided in Figure 1. Readers will find it helpful to refer to this figure during the following description of the testing criteria.

2.2.1 Product and concept tests

Tests have been devised for the products of SSADM and placed together in groupings that reflect which SSADM techniques are used to produce them. The SSADM product groupings are those listed below under 'SSADM product grouping references' and are based on the groupings in the British Standard.

Tests have also been devised for support for SSADM concepts. Concepts are the building blocks of the system model that the SSADM practitioner constructs, whether described in words or diagrammatic form. A Data Flow Diagram - Level 1, for example, is a diagram *product* containing instances of the *concepts* process, data flow, external entity, and so on.

In the questionnaire, tests for the support of concepts have been grouped with the tests for those products in which they are created. They are listed separately from product tests, for ease of testing, and so that they need only be defined once, even if occurring in more than one product.

Testing Criteria for the SSADM
Version 4 Tools Conformance Scheme

For readers who are familiar with the SSADM Version 4 Reference Manual, the placement of some tests within some groupings will be unexpected. The index in Annex A gives cross-references to the Reference Manual chapters which describe the creation of all SSADM products for which there are tests.

2.2.2 SSADM product grouping references

The SSADM product groupings used in the Conformance Scheme are listed below. The product grouping references used within the test identifiers are also listed. (Test identifiers are explained in section 2.2.7):

SSADM Product Grouping	Conformance Scheme Reference
Business System Options	BSO
Data Flow Modelling	DFM
Dialogue Design	DDN
Entity Event Modelling	EEM
Function Definition	FDF
Logical Data Modelling	LDM
Logical Database Process Design	LDP
Processing Specification	PSN
Relational Data Analysis	RDA
Requirements Definition	RDF
Specification Prototyping	SPP
Technical System Options	TSO
Physical Data Design	PDD
Physical Process Specification	PPS
Physical Environment Description	PED
Miscellaneous	MIS

2.2.3	'Miscellaneous' grouping	This grouping contains tests for products and concepts which do not fit into the other groupings. This follows the organisation of the British Standard. Two products defined by the Standard - Project Initiation Document (PID) and SSADM Structure Diagram - have no tests in the scheme. The PID is created outside the SSADM project, so support for it in SSADM CASE tools is not tested for. Elements of the SSADM Structure Diagram notation are tested for in the context of the specific products in which they are used.
2.2.4	Additional concepts	Some concepts not explicitly described in the SSADM Version 4 Reference Manual or in the British Standard have been used to ease the implementation of the scheme's testing criteria. An example is 'System'.
2.2.5	Structure of test sets	Tests are set out in a standard way for all products and concepts. This structure is described below. For brevity, products and concepts are collectively referred to in this volume as 'entities'.
	Signicance statement	The entity (product or concept) is first defined in a *significance statement* which begins to the effect that

> 'ABC1. Each **Some Entity** has significance as ...'

- followed by a definition summarising the scope and purpose of that concept. The significance statement is derived from the definitions and product definitions given in the British Standard, and helps the tester be clear which product or concept tests are listed for. The significance statement is not itself tested.

Test categories — The tests which follow are grouped within the categories given below and preceded by interrogative words in the form 'Does your software tool ensure that each **Some Entity**:

> question1?
>
> question2?
>
> question3?...'

The categories of tests are:

- *Mandatory Relationships*: for the given entity a relationship with another entity which the software tool must *enforce*

- *Optional Relationships*: for the given entity a relationship with another entity which the software tool must *allow*

- *Attributes*: a list of attributes for the given entity

- *Object Representation*: the presentation conventions for a given entity which has graphical content

- *Quality Criteria*: tests for quality, ensuring that a given entity is consistent, complete and correct.

Object Representation

For products that have graphical content, such as diagrams, the British Standard gives **preferred** presentation conventions. Conformity for individual products can be accomplished with graphical representation that differs from the 'preferred presentation', provided that the delivered products of SSADM conform in other respects, such as composition and completion criteria.

In the questionnaire, presentation conventions are tested separately as 'object representation'. Tests have been constructed only for the 'preferred' presentation conventions.

Attribute dependent tests

Tests apply to all instances of an entity, except where only relevant for a particular value of an attribute. Such tests (attribute dependent tests) are also given within the entity's test set. They are given in the form:

Where Attribute: Structure = "SEQUENCE"...

Chapter 2
The Testing Criteria Questionnaire

Tests are given for all settings of those attributes where options can be pre-defined. For example, an attribute *Structure* could have pre-defined values such as 'SEQUENCE', 'ITERATION' or 'SELECTION'. Attribute dependent tests would be given for each value and are arranged in these categories:

- *Attribute Dependent Mandatory Relationships*
- *Attribute Dependent Optional Relationships*
- *Attribute Dependent Object Representation*
- *Attribute Dependent Quality Criteria.*

2.2.6 Summary of the testing criteria structure

Figure 1 summarises the structure of the testing criteria. In figure 1 the 'multiple box' symbols indicate that a section of tests occurs a number of times. Figure 2 illustrates this.

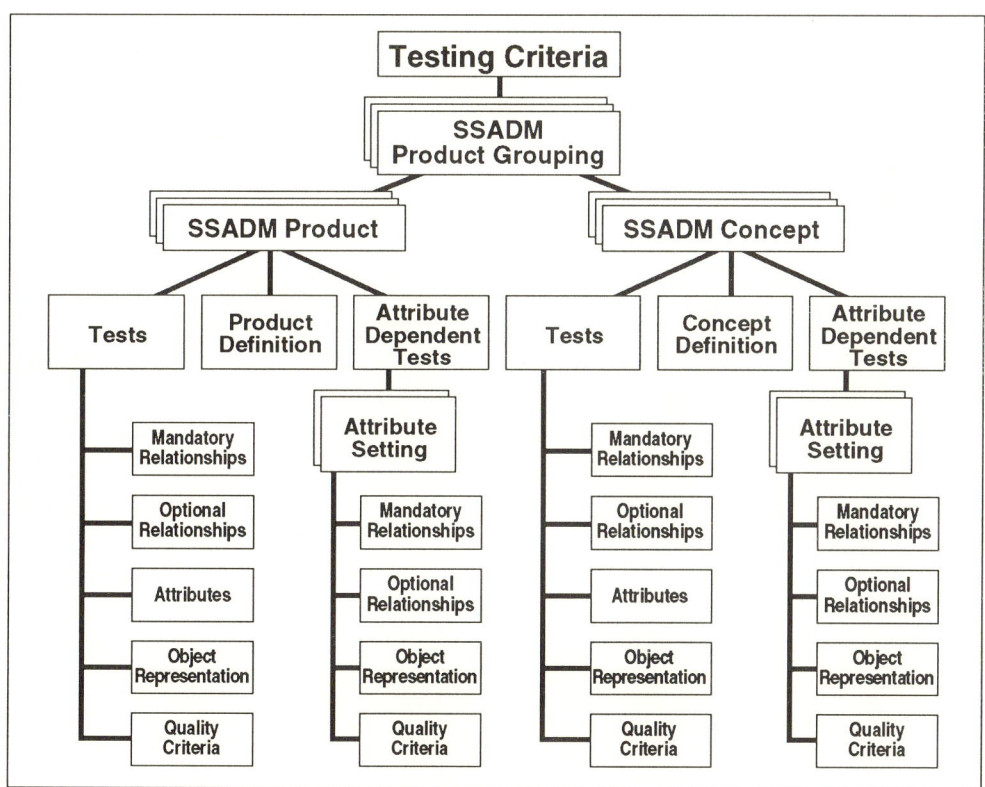

Figure 1: Structure of the Testing Criteria set

The following symbols indicate that there are multiple product groupings; within each grouping a number of products are tested, and a number of concept tests follow on from the product tests, within each product grouping.

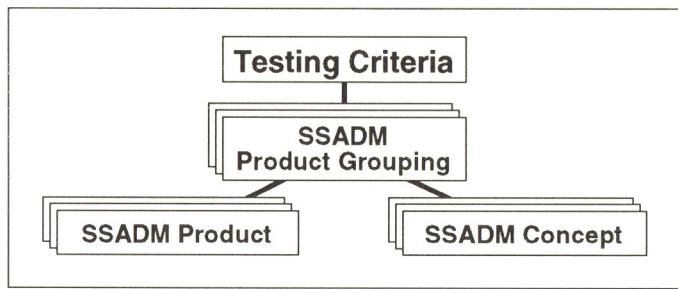

Figure 2: Multiple sections.

2.2.7 Test identifiers

Each test has a unique identifier made up of components as follows:

[AAA XX BBBB YY]

(1) (2) (3) (4)

For example:

'DFM 51 ADMR 1'

The first three characters (1) denote the product grouping for which that test is relevant. (See 'Conformance Scheme Reference' under section 2.2.2, SSADM product group references.)

The product reference is followed by a sequential number (2) :

- if the number is 50 or less, the test relates to an SSADM *product*;
- if the number is greater than 50, the test relates to an SSADM *concept*.

The above is followed by up to 4 characters (3) denoting the category of test:

MR - Mandatory Relationship

OR - Optional Relationship

> A - Attribute
>
> OB - Object Representation
>
> QC - Quality Criterion.

(Where tests are dependent on the setting of an attribute value, they test 'Attribute Dependent' rules, and are denoted ADxx):

> ADMR - Attribute Dependent Mandatory Relationship
>
> ADOR - Attribute Dependent Optional Relationship
>
> ADOB - Attribute Dependent Object Representation
>
> ADQC - Attribute Dependent Quality Criterion.

The above is followed by a sequential number (4) for each test in that category.

Thus the test identifier example given below,

> 'DFM51ADMR1'

indicates that this test relates to an SSADM concept under the data flow modelling product grouping and is the first attribute dependent rule to be listed.

2.2.8	Attribute Dependent Tests	Attribute dependent tests are prefixed by a statement in the form:

> Where Attribute: [attribute name] = [valid value for attribute]
>
> [test statement]

2.2.9	Composite tests	Some tests are composed of several logical fragments. Composite tests express the rule by which entities can be related to more than one other entity, either as alternatives (denoted by OR) or as complementary (denoted by AND).

To limit the length of text need to express each test, some tests use the shortand AND / OR. This expresses the rule that an entity may maintain a relationship to more than one other entity, or to both entities. For a tool to pass the test it must support each fragment of the logic.

2.2.10 SSADM Stage identification

Each significance statement and each test are followed by one or more SSADM Stage numbers in brackets. These denote the Stage(s) where that question is relevant. Thus if a product is created in Stage 1 and updated (or a new variant of it created) in Stage 3, then '(1,3)' will appear after the tests. A relationship to another product may only be relevant to Stage 1 however, and '(1)' will appear after the test for that relationship.

The Stage numbers enable the tool's support for each Stage to be identified and summarised in the conformance results, as explained in Chapter 3.

Attributes have not been marked with Stage numbers in the tests, for clarity: the assumption to be made is that the Stage numbers in the significance statements apply to all attributes, unless stated specifically.

3 Use of the questionnaire in appraisals

3.1 Extent of testing

There are no *mandatory requirements* in terms of SSADM support which a software tool must satisfy in the scheme, therefore there is no distinction between tests which must be passed and those that are optional. All tests must be made against the tool which is being appraised, except where the appraisal is on an agreed restricted basis to test for a limited area of support. (Refer to *A Guide to the SSADM Version 4 Tools Conformance Scheme* for a full explanation of restricted appraisals.)

Mandatory and optional relationship tests

The terms mandatory and optional do **not** mean that a software tool must pass some tests and does not have to pass others - optionality refers to the *relationships* and not to the tests.

Composite tests

A test that is a composite of fragments (logically linked by AND and OR) cannot be broken down into separate tests. This is the case in both full and restricted appraisals: in this context the term *restricted* does not mean only part of a composite test may be satisfied.

3.2 Interpetation of the questions

Before undertaking an appraisal, testers should clearly understand the wording used in the testing criteria, which is explained in the following sections.

Implementation of the rules embodied in the tests

All tests listed are implicitly for when a product is completed.

Some tools may offer completeness and consistency checking as the user is working, perhaps to the extent of forcing the user to correct inconsistencies before permitting further work: other tools may offer checking reports. (These approaches are covered in the *CASE Tools* volume of CCTA's Appraisal and Evaluation Library. The reader is referred to *A Guide to the SSADM Version 4 Tools Conformance Scheme* for further discussion on the use of the scheme results in appraisal and evaluation.) In the Conformance Scheme, either approach is deemed acceptable - the tests are valid for a SSADM product when completed at Stage or Module end.

Mandatory relationship tests	Mandatory relationship tests are preceded by the wording, in question form:
	> 'Does the software tool ensure that each **SomeEntity**... \<test>?
	Since some tools allow a SSADM entity to be held in an incomplete or an inconsistent state while work is in progress, the wording of the test for mandatory relationships may be read as:
	> 'Can the software tool detect and report contraventions of the rule that.... \<test>?
Optional relationship tests	Optional relationship tests are preceded by the wording, in question form:
	> 'Does the software tool allow each **SomeEntity**... \<test>?
	The test is a mandatory test to check that a relationship may be set up in the tool if the user requires it. Thus the tool may allow a **Resource Flow Diagram** to contain one or more **Resource Stores**. The tool must allow the resource store to be drawn in the diagram, but does not signal a completeness error if the user has not placed one on the diagram.
Relationships with entity variants	A relationship existing between one entity and another entity may only exist for a *variant* of the other entity. (Examples of 'variant' being 'Current Environment' or 'Required System', or 'Where Type = ITERATION'.) Since a relationship is tested at both 'ends' (that is, there is a test for the relationship from the master entity to the detail entity, and another from detail back to master) it would be strictly necessary to identify the variant entity in both tests. This has not been done in the test for the 'end' that is invariant - for clarity. As an example, compare
	> 'each SomeEntity is documented by one and only one NODE'
	> with

Chapter 3
Use of the Questionnaire in Appraisals

'Where Attribute : Type = 'Root' ... each NODE is in one-to-one correspondence with one and only one SomeEntity'.

In the latter, the specific variant is identified by using an Attribute Dependent test.

Attribute tests

Attribute tests are preceded by the wording:

'Does the software tool support the following attributes?'

The tester is invited by this question to tick off the attributes which the tool supports as part of the product or concept. All attributes are *mandatory*. A tool should support all attributes and earn 100% score. If some attributes are not supported this will be reflected in a lower percentage result.

Attribute validation rules

Tools may differ in how they implement the validation rule given for an attribute. The tester should be prepared to accept the tool builder's implementation if it can be seen as satisfying the rule. For example:

- where values are listed in lower case ('u / r / ru') this embraces upper case ('U / R / RU')

- where a validation such as 'BOOLEAN' is given in a test, this is to be interpreted as embracing any implementation that represents mutually exclusive alternatives ('YES/NO', 'TRUE/FALSE', '1 / 0')

and so on.

Scope of 'unique'

Where the validation of an attribute is 'unique', the scope is understood to be a development project - there is not a need for uniqueness between versions of a deliverable from that project.

The ‡ symbol

Within the list of attributes to be tested for some products or concepts the ‡ symbol appears. The symbol means the following:

15

- the attribute is actually stored as an attribute of another entity, (where it is listed in a test without the ‡ symbol)

- the attribute is merely a copy of the original attribute (hence the use of the sign ‡).

The copy attribute will be included in the attribute tests of the entity in which it is listed. (The attribute may be required for visibility in the SSADM documentation product, or for attribute dependent tests in the scheme.)

Object representation tests

Object representation tests are *mandatory*. They test the *preferred* presentation for graphical objects given in the British Standard. If a tool adopts alternative presentations it will not pass these tests.

However, this does not mean that a tool is incapable of supporting the SSADM practitioner, but that the *preferred* presentation conventions of the British Standard are not adhered to by the tool. These tests are prefaced by the wording:

> 'Does the software tool ensure that each SomeDiagrammaticEntity has the following object representation?'

Quality criteria tests

Quality criteria tests are preceded by the wording:

> 'Which of the following quality criteria does the software tool enforce:
>
> <tests>'

As with attributes, the quality criteria (which represent checks on the completeness and consistency of the SSADM products) are mandatory.

3.4 Testing process and determining results

Each test occurs in an SSADM product grouping and is identified as being relevant for one or more SSADM Stages. It is therefore possible to view the same set of results of testing from two perspectives - support for SSADM products, and support for SSADM Stages.

Chapter 3
Use of the Questionnaire in Appraisals

Product support To determine the extent of SSADM support for all product groupings, the tester will:

1. carry out all tests

2. count the 'yes' responses to tests in each product grouping, for each major category of test:

    - relationships
    - attributes
    - object representation
    - quality criteria

3. calculate the total of tests passed in that product grouping as a percentage of the number of all tests available, for each major category of test

4. present the results as outlined in Chapter 4.

Stage support Alternatively, if the requirement is to assess the extent of SSADM support for all SSADM Stages, the process would be similar to the above, replacing steps 2 and 3:

2. count the 'yes' responses to tests for each major category of test, separately counting the tests designated by each stage number (0 to 6) in turn:

    - relationships
    - attributes
    - object representation
    - quality criteria

3. calculate the total number of tests passed in that product grouping as a percentage of the number of all tests available, for each of the above four categories of test.

Testing Criteria for the SSADM
Version 4 Tools Conformance Scheme

3.5 **Use of the questionnaire**

The testing criteria have been laid out in the form of a questionnaire to help those testing tools. The questionnaire format can be used by suppliers during the registration process to declare the levels of support that their tool offers. The questionnaire can also be used in the appraisal process. Reproduction of the questionnaire is subject to the notice given on the reverse of the title page of this volume.

Testing organisations and those conducting their own appraisals are recommended to use a software tool such as a spreadsheet to facilitate the compilation of results. The numbering of the testing criteria and layout of the questionnaire will assist this compilation task.

Potential customers of CASE tools may find the layout helpful in assessing their requirements for SSADM support.

4 Presentation of results summaries and conformance certificate

4.1 General

As described in *A Guide to the SSADM Version 4 Tools Conformance Scheme,* independent testing organisations are required to publish the summaries of the results of open appraisals in a standard format to assist fair comparisons between CASE tools.

4.2 Bar Charts

When publishing summaries of Conformance Scheme results, independent testing organisations should follow a 'bar chart' layout, which gives a profile of how the CASE tool supports each product grouping and SSADM Stage.

In both views, bar charts show the results of tests for support of SSADM products for the categories of:

- relationships
- attributes
- object representation
- quality criteria

as defined in Chapter 2 of this volume.

The height of each bar and scores shown will represent tests passed, as a percentage of all possible tests in the product grouping or Stage. These are illustrated below.

(The percentages in the bar charts given here are illustrative only, and are not intended to reflect the scoring that might be achieved by a usable tool.)

Nil scores

Where a tool passes no tests in a category, the bar chart will show this explicitly with 'Nil'. Where there are no tests in a category for a product grouping (such as for those product groupings which do not have diagrammatic content, hence no object representation) this should be signified by 'N/A' (not applicable).

Testing Criteria for the SSADM
Version 4 Tools Conformance Scheme

In a restricted appraisal, where the category is unsupported this should be designated 'Not supported'. (Drawing tools, for example, may not support relationships or quality criteria).

4.3 **Conformance Certificate Information**

The Conformance Certificate awarded to a product will identify the version and hardware and software environment of the product appraised, together with the name of the testing organisation and date of the appraisal. The bar charts of product grouping and Stage support will be reproduced on the Conformance Certificate. This information will be publicly available, as described in the *Guide*.

4.4 **SSADM product group support**

Product Grouping	SSADM Product Support			
	Relationships	Attributes	Object Representation	Quality Criteria
	25% 50% 75%	25% 50% 75%	25% 50% 75%	25% 50% 75%
Business System Options	61%	61%	N/A	61%
Data Flow Modelling	82%	82%	85%	82%
Dialogue Design	47%	47%	33%	47%
Entity Event Modelling	80%	80%	70%	80%
Function Definition	53%	53%	45%	53%

Figure 4.1: Product grouping support (extract)

Chapter 4
Presentation of Results Summaries and Conformance Certificate

4.5 SSADM Stage support

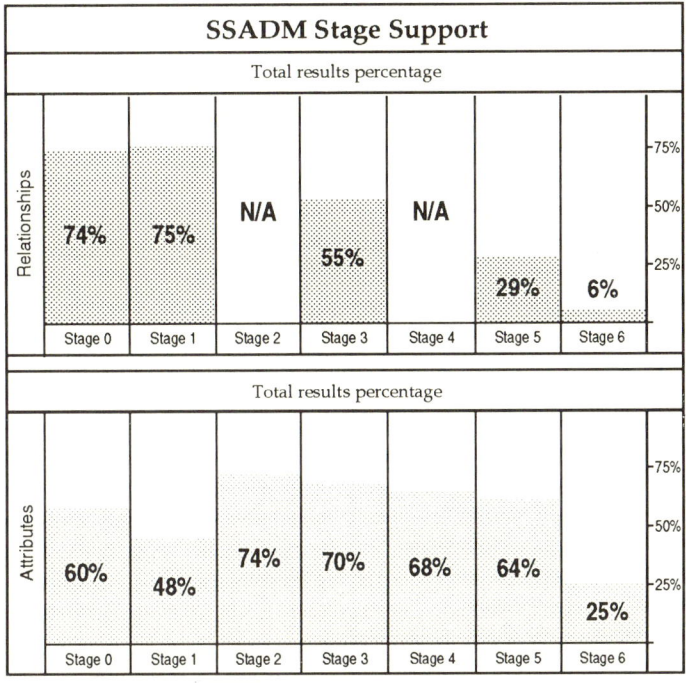

Figure 4.2: Stage support (extract)

Testing Criteria for the SSADM
Version 4 Tools Conformance Scheme

4.6 Conformance Certificate

SSADM Version 4 Tools Conformance Scheme

(Name of tool), (version number), running under (software) on (hardware configuration) conforms to SSADM as defined in (number) of the British Standard, *Specification for Information Systems Products Using SSADM*, to the following levels:

Testing Organisation: Date of appraisal:

SSADM Stage Support

Total results percentage scores

	Stage 0	Stage 1	Stage 2	Stage 3	Stage 4	Stage 5	Stage 6
Relationships	74%	75%	N/A	55%	N/A	29%	6%
Attributes	60%	48%	74%	70%	68%	64%	25%
Object Representation	74%	75%	N/A	55%	N/A	29%	6%
Quality Criteria	60%	48%	74%	70%	68%	64%	25%

Figure 4.3: The 'Conformance Certificate' showing results summaries by Stage.

Chapter 4
Presentation of Results Summaries and Conformance Certificate

SSADM Version 4 Tools Conformance Scheme

SSADM Product Support

Product Grouping	Relationships (25% 50% 75%)	Attributes (25% 50% 75%)	Object Representation (25% 50% 75%)	Quality Criteria (25% 50% 75%)
Business System Options	61%	61%	N/A	61%
Data Flow Modelling	82%	82%	85%	82%
Dialogue Design	47%	47%	33%	47%
Entity Event Modelling	80%	80%	70%	80%
Function Definition	53%	53%	45%	53%
Logical Data Modelling	78%	78%	78%	86%
Logical Database Process Design	26%	26%	50%	26%
Processing Specification	18%	18%	53%	18%
Relational Data Analysis	20%	20%	3%	20%
Requirements Definition	50%	50%	N/A	50%
Specification Prototyping	30%	30%	10%	30%
Technical System Options	62%	62%	N/A	62%
Physical Data Design	17%	17%	N/A	17%
Physical Process Specification	60%	60%	N/A	60%
Physical Environment Descriptions	13%	13%	N/A	13%
Miscellaneous Products	100%	100%	N/A	100%

Figure 4.4: The 'Conformance Certificate' showing results summaries by Product.

Part B:

Testing Criteria.

5 Business System Options

This chapter contains tests for the following products and concepts:

Products

BSO1	Business System Options	28
BSO2	Cost/Benefit Analysis	29
BSO3	Feasibility Options	30
BSO4	Impact Analysis	32
BSO5	Selected Business System Option	34
BSO6	Feasibility Report	36

Concepts

BSO51	Business System Option	37
BSO52	Feasibility Option	39

BSO1 Business System Options

Each **Business System Options** has significance as the set of Business System Options which is compiled so that a selection can be made. (2)

Mandatory Relationships	✓	Does the software tool ensure that each **Business System Options**		
BSO1MR1		Contains one or more **Business System Option**? (2)		

Optional Relationships   None

Attributes	✓	Which attributes for each **Business System Options** does the software tool support?		
		Name	Description	Validation
BSO1A1		Name	Name of Set	Unique identifier

Object Representation	✓	Does the software tool ensure that each **Business System Options** has the following object representation?
BSO1OB1		A **Business System Options** consist of A set of **Business System Option**

Quality Criteria   None

Attribute Dependent Tests

Mandatory Relationships   None

Optional Relationships   None

Object Representation   None

Quality Criteria   None

Chapter 5
Business System Options

BSO2 Cost/Benefit Analysis

Each **Cost/Benefit Analysis** has significance to present costs of a proposed option for completion of the project which are balanced against benefits, therefore assisting in the decision making process.(0,2,4)

Mandatory Relationships	✓	Does the software tool ensure that each **Cost/Benefit Analysis**
BSO2MR1		documents one and only one **Feasibility Option** (0) OR documents one and only one **Feasibility Report** (0) OR documents one and only one **Business System Option** (2) OR documents one and only one **Selected Business System Option** (2) OR documents one and only one **Technical System Option** (4) OR documents one and only one **Selected Technical System Option**? (4)

Optional Relationships   None

Attributes	✓	Which of the following attributes for each **Cost/Benefit Analysis** does the software tool support?		
		Name	Description	Validation
BSO2A1		Identifier	Name/id of option	Name/id of existing option
BSO2A2		Description	Description of Costs/Benefits	Text

Object Representation	✓	Does the software tool ensure that each **Cost/ Benefit Analysis** has the following object representation?
BSO2OB1		Any textual representation

Quality Criteria   None

Attribute Dependent Tests

Mandatory Relationships   None

Optional Relationships   None

Object Representation   None

Quality Criteria   None

BSO3 Feasibility Options

Each **Feasibility Options** has significance as the set of Feasibility Options which is to be considered, during a feasibility study, in selecting the way ahead. (0)

Mandatory Relationships	✓	Does the software tool ensure that each **Feasibility Options**
BSO3MR1		contains one or more **Feasibility Option**? (0)
BSO3MR2		is the basis for one and only one **Feasibility Report**? (0)

Optional Relationships   None

Chapter 5
Business System Options

Attributes	✓	Which of the following attributes for each **Feasibility Options** does the software tool support?		
		Name	**Description**	**Validation**
BSO3A1		Name	Name of Set	Unique identifier

Object Representation	✓	Does the software tool ensure that each **Feasibility Options** has the following object representation?
BSO3OB1		A **Feasibility Options** consists of a set of **Feasibility Option**

Quality Criteria   None

Attribute Dependent Tests

Mandatory Relationships   None

Optional Relationships   None

Object Representation   None

Quality Criteria   None

31

Testing Criteria for the SSADM
Version 4 Tools Conformance Scheme

BSO4 Impact Analysis

Each **Impact Analysis** has significance as describing the effects of the option (feasibility, business or technical) on the user environment and will cover issues concerned with organisation, procedures and implementation factors. This product is used to document the ramifications of pursuing a particular course of action. (0,2,4)

Mandatory Relationships	✓	Does the software tool ensure that each **Impact Analysis**
BSO4MR1		documents one and one only **Feasibility Option** (0) OR documents one and one only **Feasibility Report** (0) OR documents one and one only **Business System Option** (2) OR documents one and one only **Selected Business System Option** (2) OR documents one and one only **Technical System Option** (4) OR documents one and one only **Selected Technical System Option** (4) OR documents one and one only **Technical Environment Description**? (4)

Optional Relationships	✓	Does the software tool allow an **Impact Analysis**
BSO4OR1		to be supported by one and one only **Take-On Requirements Description**? (4)
BSO4OR2		to be supported by one and one only **Training Requirements Description**? (4)
BSO4OR3		to be supported by one and one only **User Manual Requirements Description**? (4)

Chapter 5
Business System Options

Attributes	✓	Which of the following attributes for each **Impact Analysis** does the software tool support?		
		Name	**Description**	**Validation**
BSO4A1		Identifier	Name/id of option	Name/id of existing option
BSO4A2		Description	Description of Impact	Text

Object Representation   None

Quality Criteria   None

Attribute Dependent Tests

Mandatory Relationships   None

Optional Relationships   None

Object Representation   None

Quality Criteria   None

BSO5 Selected Business System Option

Each **Selected Business System Option** has significance to document the option chosen to provide the description of system functionality so that further work can be done to develop the Requirements Specification. (2) (4)

Mandatory Relationships	✓	Does the software tool ensure that each **Selected Business System Option**
BSO5MR1		is based on one or more **Business System Option**? (2)
BSO5MR2		is the basis for one or more **Technical System Option**? (4)

Optional Relationships	✓	Does the software tool allow a **Selected Business System Option**
BSO5OR1		to be documented by one and only one **Data Flow Diagram - Level 1**? (2)
BSO5OR2		to be documented by one or more **Data Flow Diagram - Lower Level**? (2)
BSO5OR3		to be documented by one and only one **Logical Data Structure**? (2)
BSO5OR4		to be documented by one and only one **Cost/Benefit Analysis**? (2)
BSO5OR5		to be documented by one and only one **Impact Analysis**? (2)

Chapter 5
Business System Options

Attributes	✓	Which of the following attributes for each **Selected Business System Option** does the software tool support?		
		Name	Description	Validation
BSO5A1		Identifier	ID of selected option	Unique
BSO5A2		Description	Description of selected option	Text

Object Representation   None

Quality Criteria   None

Attribute Dependent Tests

Mandatory Relationships   None

Optional Relationships   None

Object Representation   None

Quality Criteria   None

Testing Criteria for the SSADM
Version 4 Tools Conformance Scheme

BSO6 Feasibility Report

Each **Feasibility Report** has significance as the module product from the Feasibility Study Module. It documents the possible approaches to the system development and assesses the impact of each so that the most appropriate way ahead can be fully investigated. (0)

Mandatory Relationships	✓	Does the software tool ensure that each **Feasibility report**
BSO6MR1		is based on one and only one **Feasibility Options**? (0)

Optional Relationships	✓	Does the software tool allow a **Feasibility Report**
BSO6OR1		to be documented by one and only one **Data Flow Diagram - Level 1**? (0)
BSO6OR2		to be documented by one or more **Data Flow Diagram - Lower Level**? (0)
BSO6OR3		to be documented by one and only one **Logical Data Structure**? (0)
BSO6OR4		to be documented by one and only one **Cost/Benefit Analysis**? (0)
BSO6OR5		to be documented by one and only one **Impact Analysis**? (0)

Attributes	✓	Which of the following attributes for each **Feasibility Report** does the software tool support?		
		Name	Description	Validation
BSO6A1		Identifier	ID of report	Unique
BSO6A2		Content	Content of report	Text

Chapter 5
Business System Options

Object Representation   None

Quality Criteria   None

Attribute Dependent Tests

Mandatory Relationships   None

Optional Relationships   None

Object Representation   None

Quality Criteria   None

BSO51 Business System Option

Each **Business System Option** has significance as presenting a high-level system design containing descriptions of the functional areas to be included in the system (ie encompassed by the system boundary), the requirements to be addressed, and the potential impact on the organisation. (2)

Mandatory Relationships	✓	Does the software tool ensure that each **Business Systems Option**
BSO51MR1		belongs to one and only one **Business System Option**? (2)

37

Optional Relationships	✓	Does the software tool allow a **Business System Option**
BSO51OR1		to be a basis for one and only one **Selected Business System Option**? (2)
BSO51OR2		to be documented by one and only one **Data Flow Diagram - Level 1**? (2)
BSO51OR3		to be documented by one or more **Data Flow Diagram - Lower Level** ? (2)
BSO51OR4		to be documented by one and only one **Logical Data Structure**? (2)
BSO51OR5		to be documented by one and only one **Cost/Benefit Analysis**? (2)
BSO51OR6		to be documented by one and only one **Impact Analysis**? (2)

Attributes	✓	Which of the following attributes for each **Business System Option** does the software tool support?		
		Name	Description	Validation
BSO51A1		Identifier	Number/Name	Unique ID
BSO51A2		Description	Description of option	Text

Object Representation   None

Quality Criteria   None

Chapter 5
Business System Options

Attribute Dependent Tests

Mandatory Relationships   None

Optional Relationships   None

Object Representation   None

Quality Criteria   None

BSO52 Feasibility Option

Each **Feasibility Option** has significance as documenting the functions to be incorporated and details implementation requirements. (0)

Mandatory Relationships	✓	Does the software tool ensure that each **Feasibility Option**
BSO52MR1		belongs to one and only one **Feasibility Options**? (0)

Optional Relationships	✓	Does the software tool allow a **Feasibility Option**
BSO52OR1		to be augmented by one and only one **Data Flow Model**? (0)
BSO52OR2		to be augmented by one and only one **Logical Data Model**? (0)
BSO52OR3		to be documented by one and only one **Cost/Benefit Analysis**? (0)
BSO52OR4		to be documented by one and only one **Impact Analysis**? (0)

Testing Criteria for the SSADM
Version 4 Tools Conformance Scheme

Attributes	✓	Which of the following attributes for each **Feasibility Option** does the software tool support?		
		Name	Description	Validation
BSO52A1		Identifier	Number/Name	Unique ID
BSO52A2		Description	Description of option	Text

Object Representation   None

Quality Criteria   None

Attribute Dependent Tests

Mandatory Relationships   None

Optional Relationships   None

Object Representation   None

Quality Criteria   None

Chapter 6
Data Flow Modelling

6 Data Flow Modelling

This chapter contains tests for the following products and concepts:

Products

DFM1	Context Diagram	42
DFM2	Data Flow Diagram - Level 1	43
DFM3	Data Flow Diagram - Lower Level	45
DFM4	Data Flow Model	47
DFM5	Document Flow Diagram	50
DFM6	Elementary Process Description	51
DFM7	External Entity Description	53
DFM8	I/O Descriptions	54
DFM9	Logical Data Store/Entity Cross-Reference	55
DFM10	not used	
DFM11	Logical/Physical Data Store Cross-Reference	57
DFM12	not used	
DFM13	Process/Entity Matrix	58
DFM14	not used	
DFM15	Resource Flow Diagram	59

Concepts

DFM51	DFD Process	61
DFM52	Data Store	64
DFM53	External Entity	68
DFM54	Data Flow	71
DFM55	Resource Store	75
DFM56	Resource Flow	76
DFM57	Document Flow	78
DFM58	System	79
DFM59	Common Process	80
DFM60	Logical Data Store/Entity Cross-Reference Detail	82
DFM61	Logical/Physical Data Store Cross-Reference Detail	83
DFM62	Process/Entity Matrix Entry	84

Testing Criteria for the SSADM
Version 4 Tools Conformance Scheme

DFM1 Context Diagram

Each **Context Diagram** has significance as illustrating the initial scope of the proposed system, and concentrates on the major inputs and outputs of the system and shows the external sources and recipients of system data.(0,1)

Mandatory Relationships | ✓ | Does the software tool ensure that each **Context Diagram**

DFM1MR1	belongs to one and only one **Current Services Description**? (1)
DFM1MR2	contains one or more **External Entity**? (0,1)
DFM1MR3	contains one or more **Data Flow**? (0,1)
DFM1MR4	highlights the scope for one and only one **System**? (0,1)

Optional Relationships   None

Attributes | ✓ | Which of the following attributes for each **Context Diagram** does the software tool support?

	Name	Description	Validation
DFM1A1	Name	Name of the Diagram	Unique Identifier

Object Representation | ✓ | Does the software tool ensure that each **Context Diagram** has the following object representation?

DFM1OB1	A **Context Diagram** is composed of • System • External Entity • Data Flow

Quality Criteria   None

Chapter 6
Data Flow Modelling

Attribute Dependent Tests

Mandatory Relationships   None

Optional Relationships   None

Object Representation   None

Quality Criteria   None

DFM2 Data Flow Diagram - Level 1

Each **Data Flow Diagram - Level 1** has significance as containing the overall information flow model of the system, and an abstract view of the processes and scope of the system being described.(0,1,2,3)

Mandatory Relationships	✓	Does the software tool ensure that each **Data Flow Diagram - Level 1**
DFM2MR1		is a component of one and only one **Data Flow Model**? (0,1,3) OR documents one and only one **Selected Business System Option**? (2) OR documents one and only one **Business System Option**? (2) OR documents one and only one **Feasibility Report**? (0)
DFM2MR2		contains one or more **DFD Process**? (0,1,3)
DFM2MR3		contains one or more **External Entity**? (0,1,3)
DFM2MR4		contains one or more **Data Flow**? (0,1,3)

Testing Criteria for the SSADM
Version 4 Tools Conformance Scheme

Optional Relationships	✓	Does the software tool allow a **Data Flow Diagram - Level 1**		
DFM2OR1		to contain one or more **Data Store**? (0,1,3)		
DFM2OR2		to contain one or more **Resource Store**? (0,1,3)		
DFM2OR3		to contain one or more **Resource Flow**? (0,1,3)		

Attributes	✓	Which of the following attributes for each **Data Flow Diagram - Level 1** does the software tool support?		
		Name	Description	Validation
DFM2A1		Name	Name of the Diagram	Unique Identifier

Object Representation	✓	Does the software tool ensure that each **Data Flow Diagram - Level 1** has the following object representation?
DFM2OB1		A **Data Flow Diagram - Level 1** is composed of • **DFD Process** • **External Entity** • **Data Flow** • **Data Store** • **Resource Store** • **Resource Flow**

Quality Criteria   None

Attribute Dependent Tests

Mandatory Relationships   None

Optional Relationships   None

Object Representation   None

Quality Criteria   None

Chapter 6
Data Flow Modelling

DFM3 Data Flow Diagram - Lower Level

Each **Data Flow Diagram - Lower Level** has significance as providing detailed information by describing the processes on higher level Data Flow Diagrams in more detail. The higher level may be the Level 1 Data Flow Diagram, or may be itself a Lower Level Data Flow Diagram. (1,2,3)

Mandatory Relationships	✓	Does the software tool ensure that each **Data Flow Diagram - Lower Level**
DFM3MR1		describes one and only one **Data Flow Model**? (1,3) OR documents one and only one **Selected Business System Option**? (2) OR documents one and only one **Business System Option**? (2) OR documents one and only one **Feasibility Report**? (2)
DFM3MR2		describes one and only one **DFD Process**? (1,3)
DFM3MR3		contains one or more **DFD Process**? (1,3)
DFM3MR4		contains one or more **Data Flow**? (1,3)

Optional Relationships	✓	Does the software tool allow a **Data Flow Diagram - Lower Level**
DFM3OR1		to contain one or more **External Entity**? (1,3)
DFM3OR2		to contain one or more **Data Store**? (1,3)
DFM3OR3		to contain one or more **Resource Store**? (1,3)
DFM3OR4		to contain one or more **Resource Flow**? (1,3)

Testing Criteria for the SSADM
Version 4 Tools Conformance Scheme

Attributes	✓	Which of the following attributes for each **Data Flow Diagram - Lower Level** does the software tool support?		
		Name	Description	Validation
DFM3A1		Name	Name of the Diagram	Unique Identifier
DFM3A2		Level-ID	DFD hierarchy Level No	Cardinal

Object Representation	✓	Does the software tool ensure that each **Data Flow Diagram - Lower Level** has the following object representation?
DFM3OB1		A **Data Flow Diagram - Lower Level** is composed of • **DFD Process** • **External Entity** • **Data Flow** • **Data Store** • **Resource Store** • **Resource Flow** • **Process Boundary Box**

Quality Criteria	✓	Which of the following quality criteria does the software tool enforce?
DFM3QC1		Is the boundary of the process accurately displayed? That is all objects connected to the exploded process from the parent data flow diagram (and nothing else) are displayed outside the process boundary box (1,2,3)

Attribute Dependent Tests

Mandatory Relationships   None

Optional Relationships   None

Object Representation   None

Quality Criteria   None

DFM4 Data Flow Model

Each **Data Flow Model** has significance as a set of Data Flow Diagrams and their associated documentation. The diagrams form a hierarchy with the Data Flow Diagram Level 1 showing the scope of the system and the lower level diagrams expanding the detail as appropriate. Additional documentation provides a description of the processes, input / output data flows and external entities.(0,1,3)

Mandatory Relationships	✓	Does the software tool ensure that each **Data Flow Model**
DFM4MR1		contains one and only one **Data Flow Diagram - Level 1**? (0,1,3)
DFM4MR2		contains one or more **External Entity Description**? (1,3)
DFM4MR3		contains one or more **Elementary Process Description**? (1,3)
DFM4MR4		contains <u>two</u> or more **I/O Description**? (1,3)
DFM4MR5		describes one and only one **System**? (0,1)

Optional Relationships	✓	Does the software tool allow a **Data Flow Model**
DFM4OR1		to contain one or more **Data Flow Diagram - Lower Level**? (1,3)
DFM4OR2		to augment one or more **Feasibility Option**? (0)

Testing Criteria for the SSADM
Version 4 Tools Conformance Scheme

Attributes	✓	Which of the following attributes for each **Data Flow Model** does the software tool support?		
		Name	Description	Validation
DFM4A1		Name	Name of the DFM	Unique Identifier
DFM4A2		Variant	Type of DFM	Current Physical/ Logical/Required System

Object Representation	✓	Does the software tool ensure that each **Data Flow Model** has the following object representation?
DFM4OB1		A **Data Flow Model** is composed of • Data Flow Diagram - Level 1 • Data Flow Diagram - Lower Level • Elementary Process Description • External Entity Description • I/O Description

Quality Criteria	✓	Which of the following quality criteria does the software tool enforce?
DFM3QC1		Are all external entities, stores, and flows represented consistently between levels of Data Flow Diagrams? (0,1,3)
DFM3QC2		Are process identifiers and names consistent between the DFDs and elementary process descriptions? (0,1,3)
DFM3QC3		Are all elementary flows crossing the system boundary documented using I/O descriptions? (0,1,3)
DFM3QC4		Is the location attribute on a process omitted during logicalisation? (1)
DFM3QC5		Are all resource stores and resource flows omitted during logicalisation? (1)
DFM3QC6		Have all the elementary and common processes been described in the Elementary Process Description? (1,3)
DFM3QC7		Are any data flows connecting a data store to/from another data store highlighted/rejected? (0,1,3)
DFM3QC8		Are any data flows connecting a data store to/from an external entity highlighted/rejected? (0,1,3)

Quality Criteria (cont)	✓	Which of the following quality criteria does the software tool enforce?
DFM3QC9		Are any data flows connecting a resource store to/from another data store highlighted/rejected? (0,1,3)
DFM3QC10		Are any data flows connecting a resource store to/from an external entity highlighted/rejected? (0,1,3)
DFM3QC11		Are any data/resource/document flows that are sourced by and received by the same DFD node highlighted/rejected? (0,1,3)
DFM3QC12		Are resource flows only drawn between processes and resource stores? (0,1,3)
DFM3QC13		Is the levelling of identifiers correct? (0,1,3)
DFM3QC14		Do all process identifiers use the correct notation? (0,1,3)
DFM3QC15		Do all data store identifiers use the correct notation? (0,1,3)
DFM3QC16		Do all external entity identifiers use the correct notation? (0,1,3)

Attribute Dependent Tests

Where attribute: Variant = "LOGICAL"

Mandatory Relationships	✓	Does the software tool ensure that each **Data Flow Model**
DFM4ADMR1		belongs to one and only one Current Services Description? (1)

Optional Relationships   None

Object Representation   None

Quality Criteria   None

Testing Criteria for the SSADM
Version 4 Tools Conformance Scheme

DFM5 Document Flow Diagram

Each **Document Flow Diagram** has significance as showing how documents pass around the system. (1)

Mandatory Relationships	✓	Does the software tool ensure that each **Document Flow Diagram**
DFM5MR1		contains one or more **Document Flow**? (1)
DFM5MR2		contains one or more **External Entity**? (1)
DFM5MR3		contains one or more **Data Flow**? (1)

Optional Relationships   None

Attributes	✓	Which of the following attributes for each **Document Flow Diagram** does the software tool support?		
		Name	Description	Validation
DFM5A1		Name	Name of the Diagram	Unique Identifier

Object Representation	✓	Does the software tool ensure that each **Document Flow Diagram** has the following object representation?
DFM5OB1		A **Document Flow Diagram** is composed of • **Document Flow** • **External Entity** • **Data Flow**

Quality Criteria   None

Attribute Dependent Tests

Mandatory Relationships   None

Chapter 6
Data Flow Modelling

Optional Relationships   None

Object Representation   None

Quality Criteria   None

DFM6 Elementary Process Description

Each **Elementary Process Description** has significance as describing the business environment in which the process is trying to operate. A requirement for common processing may also be described within an **Elementary Process Description** and cross referenced to the elementary processes of functions which use it. (1,3)

Mandatory Relationships	✓	Does the software tool ensure that each **Elementary Process Description**
DFM6MR1		describes one and only one **DFD Process** (1,3) OR describes one and only one **Common Process**? (1,3)

Optional Relationships	✓	Does the software tool allow a **Elementary Process Description**
DFM6OR1		to contain one and only one **Data Flow Model**? (1,3)
DFM6OR2		to reference one or more **Common Process**? (1,3)

51

Attributes	✓	Which of the following attributes for each **Elementary Process Description** does the software tool support?		
		Name	Description	Validation
DFM6A1		Identifier	ID of the Process	ID of the elementary Process or Common Processing References
DFM6A2		Name	Name of the Process	Name of the Process
DFM6A3		Description	Description of the Process	Text
DFM6A4		Common	Common process flag	Boolean

Object Representation   None

Quality Criteria   None

Attribute Dependent Tests

Where attribute: Common = "TRUE"

Mandatory Relationships	✓	Does the software tool ensure that each **Elementary Process description**
DFM6ADMR1		belongs to one and only one **Function Definitions**? (3)

Optional Relationships   None

Object Representation   None

Quality Criteria   None

Chapter 6
Data Flow Modelling

DFM7 External Entity Description

Each **External Entity Description** has significance as explaining the relevance of an external entity in relation to the existing or proposed system. (1,3)

Mandatory Relationships	✓	Does the software tool ensure that each **External Entity Description**		
DFM7MR1		describes one and only one **External Entity**?(1,3)		
DFM7MR2		belongs to one and only one **Data Flow Model**? (1,3)		

Optional Relationships   None

Attributes	✓	Which of the following attributes for each **External Entity Description** does the software tool support?		
		Name	Description	Validation
DFM7A1		Identifier	ID of the External Entity	ID of existing External Entity
DFM7A2		Name	Name of the External Entity	Name of existing External Entity
DFM7A3		Description	Description of the External Entity	Text

Object Representation   None

Quality Criteria   None

Attribute Dependent Tests

Mandatory Relationships   None

Optional Relationships   None

Testing Criteria for the SSADM
Version 4 Tools Conformance Scheme

Object Representation None

Quality Criteria None

DFM8 I/O Descriptions

Each **I/O Descriptions** has significance as documenting all elementary data flows which cross the Data Flow Model system boundary. (1,3)

Mandatory Relationships	✓	Does the software tool ensure that each **I/O Descriptions**
DFM8MR1		describes one and only one **Data Flow**? (1,3)
DFM8MR2		belongs to one and only one **Data Flow Model**? (1,3)
DFM8MR3		contains one or more **Attribute Type**? (1,3)
DFM8MR4		is referenced by one ore more **Function Definition**? (3)

Optional Relationships None

Attributes	✓	Which of the following attributes for each **I/O Descriptions** does the software tool support?		
		Name	Description	Validation
DFM8A1		Identifier	ID of data flow	ID of existing data flow
DFM8A2		Data Content	List of attribute types	IDs of existing attribute types
DFM8A3		Comments	Note	Text

Object Representation None

Chapter 6
Data Flow Modelling

Quality Criteria	✓	Which of the following quality criteria does the software tool enforce?
DFM8QC1		Have all the data flows that cross the system boundary been described? (1,3)
DFM8QC2		Are only data flows which cross the system boundary described? (1,3)

Attribute Dependent Tests

Mandatory Relationships   None

Optional Relationships   None

Object Representation   None

Quality Criteria   None

DFM9 Logical Data Store/Entity Cross-Reference

Each **Logical Data Store/Entity Cross-Reference** has significance as a matrix showing the correspondence between logical data stores in the Data Flow Model and entities on the Logical Data Model. This is used to ensure that a main data store corresponds to an entity or group of entities. Also each entity on the Logical Data Model must be held completely within one and only one main data store. (1,3)

Mandatory Relationships	✓	Does the software tool ensure that each **Logical Data Store/Entity Cross-Reference**
DFM9MR1		belongs to one and only one **Current Services Description**?(1)
DFM9MR2		contains one or more **Logical Data Store/Entity Cross-Reference Detail**? (1,3)

55

Testing Criteria for the SSADM
Version 4 Tools Conformance Scheme

Optional Relationships   None

Attributes | ✓ | Which of the following attributes for each **Logical Data Store/Entity Cross-Reference** does the software tool support? |

DFM9A1	Name	Description	Validation
	Name	Name of the Document	Unique ID

Object Representation   None

Quality Criteria | ✓ | Which of the following quality criteria does the software tool enforce? |

DFM9QC1	Are all logical data stores defined in terms of entities? (1,3)
DFM9QC2	Do any logical data stores appear more than once within the documentation? (1,3)

Attribute Dependent Tests

Mandatory Relationships   None

Optional Relationships   None

Object Representation   None

Quality Criteria   None

Chapter 6
Data Flow Modelling

DFM11 Logical/Physical Data Store Cross-Reference

Each **Logical/Physical Data Store Cross-Reference** has significance as showing the correspondence between the logical view of data organisation and the current (physical) services. (1)

Mandatory Relationships	✓	Does the software tool ensure that each **Logical/Physical Data Store Cross-Reference**
DFM11MR1		contains one or more **Logical/Physical Data Store Cross-Reference Detail**? (1)

Optional Relationships   None

Attributes	✓	Which of the following attributes for each **Logical Data Store/Entity Cross-Reference Detail** does the software tool support?		
		Name	Description	Validation
DFM11A1		Name	Name of the Document	Unique ID

Object Representation   None

Quality Criteria	✓	Which of the following quality criteria does the software tool enforce?
DFM11QC1		Have all physical data stores been mapped to logical data stores? (1)
DFM11QC2		Are any data stores represented transient? (1)

Attribute Dependent Tests

Mandatory Relationships   None

Optional Relationships   None

Object Representation   None

Quality Criteria   None

DFM13 Process/Entity Matrix

Each **Process/Entity Matrix** has significance as cross-checking that all entities are used as the basic information for at least one process and to identify groupings of bottom-level processes during logicalisation of the Data Flow Model. (1)

Mandatory Relationships	✓	Does the software tool ensure that each **Process/Entity Matrix**
DFM13MR1		contains one or more **Process/Entity Matrix Entry**? (1)

Optional Relationships   None

Attributes	✓	Which of the following attributes for each **Process/Entity Matrix** does the software tool support?		
		Name	Description	Validation
DFM13A1		Name	Name of the Matrix	Unique ID

Object Representation   None

Chapter 6
Data Flow Modelling

Quality Criteria	✓	Which of the following quality criteria does the software tool enforce?
DFM13QC1		Are all the entities from the Logical Data Model represented on the Process/Entity Matrix? (1)
DFM13QC2		Are all bottom level processes represented on the Process/Entity Matrix? (1)
DFM13QC3		Are data flows which access a main logical data store matched by a correct entry in the matrix? (1)

Attribute Dependent Tests

Mandatory Relationships   None

Optional Relationships   None

Object Representation   None

Quality Criteria   None

DFM15 Resource Flow Diagram

Each **Resource Flow Diagram** has significance as showing how resources (physical goods) move within an organisation. (1)

Mandatory Relationships	✓	Does the software tool ensure that each **Resource Flow Diagram**
DFM15MR1		contains one or more **Resource Flow**? (1)

59

Testing Criteria for the SSADM
Version 4 Tools Conformance Scheme

Optional Relationships	✓	Does the software tool allow a **Resource Flow Diagram**		
DFM15OR1		to contain one or more **Resource Store**? (1)		
DFM15OR2		to contain one or more **DFD Process**? (1)		
DFM15OR3		to contain one or more **External Entity**? (1)		

Attributes	✓	Which of the following attributes for each **Resource Flow Diagram** does the software tool support?		
		Name	Description	Validation
DFM15A1		Name	Name of the Diagram	Unique Identifier

Object Representation	✓	Does the software tool ensure that each **Resource Flow Diagram** has the following object representation?
DFM15OB1		A **Resource Flow Diagram** is composed of • DFD Process • External Entity • Resource Flow • Resource Store

Quality Criteria   None

Attribute Dependent Tests

Mandatory Relationships   None

Optional Relationships   None

Object Representation   None

Quality Criteria   None

Chapter 6
Data Flow Modelling

DFM51 DFD Process

Each **DFD Process** has significance as a transformer or manipulator of data or physical objects. (0,1,3)

Mandatory Relationships	✓	Does the software tool ensure that each **DFD Process**
DFM51MR1		is the source of one or more **Data Flow**? (0,1,3) AND/OR is the source of one or more **Resource Flow**? (0,1,3)
DFM51MR2		is the destination for one or more **Data Flow**? (0,1,3) AND/OR is the destination for one or more **Resource Flow**? (0,1,3)

Optional Relationships	✓	Does the software tool allow a **DFD Process**
DFM51OR1		to be part of one and only one **Data Flow Diagram - Level 1**? (0,1,3)
DFM51OR2		to be part of one and only one **Resource Flow Diagram**? (1)

Attributes	✓	Which of the following attributes for each **DFD Process** does the software tool support?		
		Name	Description	Validation
DFM51A1		Identifier	ID of the Process	Unique Identifier Diagram ID + decimal extension
DFM51A2		Name	Description of the Process	Unique
DFM51A3		Location	Where the Process is performed	Text
DFM51A4		Type	Type of Process	Elementary/ Composite

61

Testing Criteria for the SSADM
Version 4 Tools Conformance Scheme

Object Representation	✓	Does the software tool ensure that each **DFD Process** has the following object representation?
DFM51OB1		Identifier ── Location / Process Description

Quality Criteria   None

Attribute Dependent Tests

Where Attribute: Type = "ELEMENTARY"

Mandatory Relationships	✓	Does the software tool ensure that each **DFD Process**
DFM51ADMR1		is part of one and only one **Data Flow Diagram - Level 1**? (0,1,3) OR is part of one and only one **Data Flow Diagram - Lower Level**? (1,3)
DFM51ADMR2		is described by one and only one **Elementary Process Description**? (1,3)
DFM51ADMR3		is part of one or more **Process/Entity Matrix Entry**? (1)

Where Attribute: Type = "COMPOSITE"

Mandatory Relationships	✓	Does the software tool ensure that each **DFD Process**
DFM51ADMR4		is described by one or more **Data Flow Diagram - Lower Level**? (1,3)

Chapter 6
Data Flow Modelling

Where Attribute: Type = "ELEMENTARY"

Optional Relationships	✓	Does the software tool allow a **DFD Process**
DFM51ADOR1		to be referenced by one or more **Function Definition**? (3)

Where attribute: Type = "ELEMENTARY"

Object Representation	✓	
DFM51ADOB1		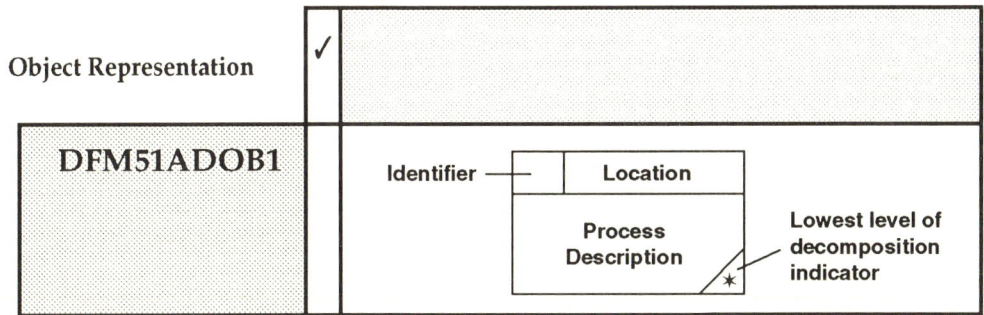

Where attribute: Type = "COMPOSITE"

Object Representation	✓	Does the software tool allow a **DFD Process** has the following object representation for the given attribute values?
DFM51ADOB2		Identifier — Location / Process Description

Where attribute: Type = "ELEMENTARY"

Quality Criteria	✓	Which of the following quality criteria does the software tool enforce?
DFM51ADQC1		Are processes that have been decomposed highlighted/rejected? (0,1,3)

63

DFM52 Data Store

Each **Data Store** has significance as a collection of any types of data in any form. (0,1,3)

Mandatory Relationships	✓	Does the software tool ensure that each **Data Store**
DFM52MR1		is generated for one and only one **Data Flow Diagram - Level 1**? (0,1,3) OR is generated for one and only one **Data Flow Diagram - Lower Level**? (1,3)
DFM52MR2		is to be the source for one or more **Data Flow**? (0,1,3)
DFM52MR3		is to be the destination for one or more **Data Flow**? (0,1,3)

Optional Relationships	✓	Does the software tool allow a **Data Store**
DFM52OR1		to be defined in terms of entities in one and only one **Logical Data Store/Entity Cross-Reference Detail**? (1,3)

Attributes	✓	Which of the following attributes for each **Data Store** does the software tool support?		
		Name	Description	Validation
DFM52A1		Identifier	ID of Data Store	Unique Diagram ID + '/' + integer
DFM52A2		Name	Description of the Data Store	Text
DFM52A3		Format	Type of Data Store	MAIN/ TRANSIENT
DFM52A4		Form	Form of Data Store	LOGICAL/ PHYSICAL
DFM52A5		Type	Type of Data Store	ELEMENTARY/ COMPOSITE

Chapter 6
Data Flow Modelling

Object Representation	✓	Does the software tool ensure that each **Data Store** has the following object representation?
DFM52OB1		Identifier ──┬── Data Store Name Identifier ──┼── Duplicated Data Store Name

Quality Criteria   None

Attribute Dependent Tests

Where attribute: Type="COMPOSITE"

Mandatory Relationships	✓	Does the software tool ensure that each **Data Store**
DFM52ADMR1		is the parent of one or more **Data Store**? (0,1,3)

Where attribute: Form = "LOGICAL"

Optional Relationships	✓	Does the software tool allow a **Data Store**
DFM52ADOR1		to be defined in terms of physical data stores in one and only one **Logical/Physical Data Store Cross-Reference Detail**? (1)

Where Attribute: Form = "PHYSICAL"

Optional Relationships	✓	Does the software tool allow a **Data Store**
DFM52ADOR2		to be defined in terms of logical data stores in one and only one **Logical/Physical Data Store Cross-Reference Detail**? (1)

Testing Criteria for the SSADM
Version 4 Tools Conformance Scheme

Where Attribute: Type = "ELEMENTARY"

Optional Relationships	✓	Does the software tool allow a **Data Store**
DFM52ADOR3		to be the child of one and only one **Data Store** ? (0,1,3)

Let Attribute: ID = '1'
Where Attribute: Format = "MAIN" and Where Attribute: Form = "LOGICAL"

Object Representation	✓	Does the software tool ensure that each **Data Store** has the following object representation?
DFM52ADOB1		The representation of the id is: D1

Where Attribute: Format = "MAIN" and Where Attribute: Form = "PHYSICAL"

Object Representation	✓	Does the software tool ensure that each **Data Store** has the following object representation?
DFM52ADOB2		The representation of the id is: M1

Where Attribute: Format = "TRANSIENT" and Where Attribute: Form = "LOGICAL"

Object Representation	✓	Does the software tool ensure that each **Data Store** has the following object representation?
DFM52ADOB3		The representation of the id is: T1

Where Attribute: Format = "TRANSIENT" and Where Attribute: Form = "PHYSICAL"

Object Representation	✓	Does the software tool ensure that each **Data Store** has the following object representation?
DFM52ADOB4		The representation of the id is: M1 (T)

Where Attribute: Type = "COMPOSITE"

Object Representation	✓	Does the software tool ensure that each **Data Store** has the following object representation?
DFM52ADOB5		Data Store 'D1' decomposes into 'D1a', 'D1b', 'D1c', etc.

Quality Criteria   None

Testing Criteria for the SSADM
Version 4 Tools Conformance Scheme

DFM53 External Entity

Each **External Entity** has significance as a source or a recipient (or both) of data and possibly also resources, which exists outside the system boundary of a defined system but which communicates with that system. (0,1,3)

Mandatory Relationships	✓	Does the software tool ensure that each **External Entity**
DFM53MR1		is described by one and only one **External Entity Description**? (1,3)
DFM53MR2		is part of one and only one **Context Diagram** (0,1) AND/OR is part of one and only one **Data Flow Diagram - Level 1** (0,1,3) AND/OR is part of one or more **Data Flow Diagram - Lower Level** (1,3) AND/OR is part of one and only one **Document Flow Diagram** (1) AND/OR is part of one and only one **Resource Flow Diagram**? (1)
DFM53MR3		is the source of one or more **Data Flow** (0,1,3) AND/OR is the source of one or more **Resource Flow** (0,1,3) AND/OR is the source of one or more **Document Flow** (1) AND/OR is the destination for one or more **Data Flow** (0,1,3) AND/OR must be the destination for one or more **Resource Flow** (0,1,3) AND/OR must be the destination for one or more **Document Flow**? (1)

Optional Relationships   None

Chapter 6
Data Flow Modelling

Attributes	✓	Which of the following attributes for each **External Entity** does the software tool support?		
		Name	Description	Validation
DFM53A1		Identifier	ID of External Entity	Unique alpha/ alphanumeric code
DFM53A2		Name	Name of External Entity	Text
DFM53A3		Type		Type of External Entity ELEMENTARY/ COMPOSITE

Object Representation	✓	Does the software tool ensure that each **External Entity** has the following object representation?
DFM53OB1		a ──── Identifier (External Entity Name) a ──── Identifier (Duplicated External Entity Name)

Quality Criteria   None

Attribute Dependent Tests

Where attribute: Type = "COMPOSITE"

Mandatory Relationships	✓	Does the software tool ensure that each **External Entity**
DFM53ADMR1		is the parent of one or more **External Entity**? (0,1,3)

69

Testing Criteria for the SSADM
Version 4 Tools Conformance Scheme

Where attribute:Type = "ELEMENTARY"

Optional Relationships	✓	Does the software tool allow each **External Entity**
DFM53ADOR1		to be the child of one and only one **External Entity**? (0,1,3)

Where attribute: Type = "COMPOSITE"

Object Representation	✓	Does the software tool ensure that each **External Entity** has the following object representation?
DFM53ADOB1		External Entity 'a' decomposes into 'a1', 'a2', 'a3', etc. (0,1,3)

Quality Criteria   None

DFM54 Data Flow

Each **Data Flow** has significance as the medium for passing data between:- a process and another process, a data store or an external entity, - two external entities. (0,1,3)

Mandatory Relationships	✓	Does the software tool ensure that each **Data Flow**
DFM54MR1		is part of one and only one **Context Diagram** (0,1) AND/OR is part of one and only one **Data Flow Diagram - Level 1** (0,1,3) AND/OR is part of one and only one **Data Flow Diagram - Lower Level** (1,3) AND/OR is part of one and only one **Document Flow Diagram** (1)
DFM54MR2		is sourced by one and only one **DFD Process**? (0,1,3) OR is sourced by one and only one **External Entity**? (0,1,3) OR is sourced by one and only one **Data Store**? (0,1,3) OR is sourced by one and only one **System**? (0,1)
DFM54MR3		is received by one and only one **DFD Process**? (0,1,3) OR is received by one and only one **External Entity**? (0,1,3) OR is received by one and only one **Data Store**? (0,1,3) OR is received by one and only one **System**? (0,1)

Testing Criteria for the SSADM
Version 4 Tools Conformance Scheme

Optional Relationships	✓	Does the software tool allow a **Data Flow**
DFM54OR1		to be referenced by one and only one **I/O Structure Description**? (3)
DFM54OR2		to be described by one and only one **I/O Structure Diagram**? (3)

Attributes		✓	Which of the following attributes for each **Data Flow** does the software tool support?		
			Name	Description	Validation
	DFM54A1		Identifier	ID of Data Flow	Unique ID
	DFM54A2		Name	Name of Data Flow	Text
	DFM54A3		Type	Type of Data Flow	COMPOSITE/ ELEMENTARY
	DFM54A4		Direction	Direction of Data Flow	ONE-WAY/ TWO-WAY
	DFM54A5		External	External Data Flow Flag	Boolean

Object Representation   None

Quality Criteria   None

Attribute Dependent Tests

Where attribute: Type="COMPOSITE"

Mandatory Relationships	✓	Does the software tool ensure that each **Data Flow**
DFM54ADMR1		is the parent of one or more **Data Flow**? (0,1,3)

Chapter 6
Data Flow Modelling

Where attribute: Type="EXTERNAL"

Mandatory Relationships	✓	Does the software tool ensure that each **Data Flow**
DFM54ADMR2		is sourced by one and only one **External Entity**? (0,1,3)
DFM54ADMR3		is received by one and only one **External Entity**? (0,1,3)

Where attribute: Type = "ELEMENTARY"

Optional Relationships	✓	Does the software tool allow a **Data Flow**
DFM54ADOR1		to be the child of one and only one **Data Flow**? (0,1,3)
DFM54ADOR2		to be the child of one and only one **I/O Description**? (0,1,3)

Where attribute: Type = "COMPOSITE"

Optional Relationships	✓	Does the software tool allow a **Data Flow**
DFM54ADOR3		to be the child of one and only one **Data Flow**? (0,1,3)

Where attribute: Direction = "ONE-WAY"

Object Representation	✓	Does the software tool ensure that each **Data Flow** has the following object representation for the given attribute values?
DFM54ADOB1		**Data Flow Name** ⟶

73

Where attribute: Direction = "TWO-WAY"

Object Representation	✓	Does the software tool ensure that each **Data Flow** has the following object representation for the given attribute values?
DFM54ADOB2		◄──── Data Flow Name ────►

Where attribute: External="TRUE"

Object Representation	✓	Does the software tool ensure that each **Data Flow** has the following object representation for the given attribute values?
DFM54ADOB3		– – – External Data Flow Name – – –►

Where attribute: Direction = "TWO-WAY"

Quality Criteria	✓	Which of the following quality criteria does the software tool enforce?
DFM51ADQC1		Are any data flows between an elementary process/data store/external entity and anything highlighted/rejected? (0,1,3)

Where attribute: Type = "ELEMENTARY"

Quality Criteria	✓	Which of the following quality criteria does the software tool enforce?
DFM51ADQC2		Attribute: Direction="ONE-WAY"

Chapter 6
Data Flow Modelling

DFM55 Resource Store

Each **Resource Store** has significance as a store of resources (not including data resources), such as goods, materials, machines, people and capital. (0,1,3)

Mandatory Relationships	✓	Does the software tool ensure that each **Resource Store**
DFM55MR1		is part of one and only one **Data Flow Diagram - Level 1** (0,1,3) AND/OR is part of one and only one **Data Flow Diagram - Lower Level** (0,1,3) AND/OR is part of one and only one **Resource Flow Diagram**? (1)
DFM55MR2		is the source of one or more **Resource Flow**? (0,1,3)
DFM55MR3		is the destination for one or more **Resource Flow**? (0,1,3)

Optional Relationships None

Attributes	✓	Which of the following attributes for each **Resource Store** does the software tool support?		
		Name	Description	Validation
DFM55A1		Name	Name of Resource Store	Text/Unique

Object Representation	✓	Does the software tool ensure that each **Resource Store** has the following object representation?
DFM55OB1		Resource Store Name

Quality Criteria None

75

Testing Criteria for the SSADM
Version 4 Tools Conformance Scheme

Attribute Dependent Tests

Mandatory Relationships   None

Optional Relationships   None

Object Representation   None

Quality Criteria   None

DFM56 Resource Flow

Each **Resource Flow** has significance as the passage of any resources except data, between: - a process and another process, a resource store or an external entity.

- two external entities. (0,1,3)

Mandatory Relationships	✓	Does the software tool ensure that each **Resource Flow**
DFM56MR1		is part of one and only one **Data Flow Diagram - Level 1** (0,1,3) AND/OR is part of one and only one **Data Flow Diagram - Lower Level** (1,3) AND/OR is part of one and only one **Resource Flow Diagram**? (0,1,3)
DFM56MR2		is sourced by one and only one **DFD Process**? (0,1,3) OR is sourced by one and only one **External Entity**? (0,1,3) OR is sourced by one and only one **Resource Store**? (0,1,3)
DFM56MR3		is received by one and only one **DFD Process**? (0,1,3) OR is received by one and only one **External Entity**? (0,1,3) OR is received by one and only one **Resource Store**? (0,1,3)

Chapter 6
Data Flow Modelling

Optional Relationships   None

Attributes	✓	Which of the following attributes for each **Resource Flow** does the software tool support?		
DFM56A1		Name	Description	Validation
		Identifier	ID of Resource Flow	Source + Destination + Name

Object Representation	✓	Does the software tool ensure that each **Resource Flow** has the following object representation?
DFM56OB1		Resource Flow ⇒

Quality Criteria   None

Attribute Dependent Tests

Mandatory Relationships   None

Optional Relationships   None

Object Representation   None

Quality Criteria   Non

77

DFM57 Document Flow

Each **Document Flow** has significance as showing the flow of physical documents within the scope of the current system. (1)

Mandatory Relationships	✓	Does the software tool ensure that each **Document Flow**	
DFM57MR1		is part of one and only one **Document Flow Diagram**? (1)	
DFM57MR2		is sourced by one and only one **External Entity**? (1)	
DFM57MR3		is received by one and only one **External Entity**? (1)	

Optional Relationships None

Attributes	✓	Which of the following attributes for each **Document Flow** does the software tool support?	
		Name	Description	Validation
DFM57A1		Name	Name of document flow	Text/Unique

Object Representation	✓	Does the software tool ensure that each **Document Flow** has the following object representation?
DFM57OB1		Document Flow Name ➤

Quality Criteria None

Attribute Dependent Tests

Mandatory Relationships None

Optional Relationships None

Chapter 6
Data Flow Modelling

Object Representation   None

Quality Criteria   None

DFM58 System

Each **System** has significance as a set of inter-related processes for the creation, maintenance, manipulation and retrieval of data. (0,1)

Mandatory Relationships	✓	Does the software tool ensure that each **System**
DFM58MR1		has its scope described by one and only one **Context Diagram**? (0,1)

Optional Relationships   None

Attributes	✓	Which of the following attributes for each **System** does the software tool support?		
		Name	Description	Validation
DFM58A1		Name	Name of system	Text/Unique

Object Representation	✓	Does the software tool ensure that each **System** has the following object representation?
DFM58OB1		System Name

Quality Criteria	✓	Which of the following quality criteria does the software tool enforce?
DFM58QC1		Is the system name unique? (0,1)

79

Testing Criteria for the SSADM
Version 4 Tools Conformance Scheme

Attribute Dependent Tests

Mandatory Relationships   None

Optional Relationships   None

Object Representation   None

Quality Criteria   None

DFM59 Common Process

Each **Common Process** has significance to be an aspect of processing which is identified as common to several processes (or functions) within an SSADM system specification. (1,3)

Mandatory Relationships	✓	Does the software tool ensure that each **Common Process**
DFM59MR1		is described by one or more **Elementary Process Description**? (1,3)

Optional Relationships	✓	Does the software tool allow a **Common Process**
DFM59OR1		to be referenced by one or more **Elementary Process Description**? (1,3)
DFM59OR2		to be referenced by one or more **Function Definition**? (1,3)

Chapter 6
Data Flow Modelling

Attributes		✓	Which of the following attributes for each **Common Process** does the software tool support?		
			Name	Description	Validation
	DFM59A1		Name	Name of the Process	Unique Identifier
	DFM59A2		Description	Description of the Process	Text

Object Representation   None

Quality Criteria   None

Attribute Dependent Tests

Mandatory Relationships   None

Optional Relationships   None

Object Representation   None

Quality Criteria   None

DFM60 Logical Data Store/Entity Cross-Reference Detail

Each **Logical Data Store/Entity Cross-Reference Detail** has significance as showing the correspondence between a logical data store in the Data Flow Model and entities on the Logical Data Model. (1,3)

Mandatory Relationships	✓	Does the software tool ensure that each **Logical Data Store/Entity Cross-Reference Detail**
DFM60MR1		contains one and only one **Data Store**? (1,3)
DFM60MR2		contains one or more **Entity Type**? (1,3)
DFM60MR3		belongs to one or more **Logical Data Store/Entity Cross-Reference**? (1,3)

Optional Relationships   None

Attributes	✓	Which of the following attributes for each **Logical Data Store/Entity Cross-Reference Detail** does the software tool support?		
		Name	Description	Validation
DFM60A1		Data Store ID	ID of Data Store	ID of existing Data Store‡
DFM60A2		Entity Name	Entity names or name	Names of existing entities

Object Representation   None

Quality Criteria   None

Attribute Dependent Tests

Mandatory Relationships   None

Chapter 6
Data Flow Modelling

Optional Relationships   None

Object Representation   None

Quality Criteria   None

DFM61 Logical/Physical Data Store Cross-Reference Detail

Each **Logical/Physical Data Store Cross-Reference Detail** has significance as showing the correspondence between the logical view of data organisation and the current (physical) services, by cross-referencing a logical data store against physical data stores. (1)

Mandatory Relationships	✓	Does the software tool ensure that each **Logical/Physical Data Store Cross-Reference Detail**
DFM61MR1		contains one and only one **Data Store**? (1)
DFM61MR2		contains one or more **Data Store**? (1)
DFM61MR3		belongs to one and only one **Logical/Physical Data Store Cross-Reference**? (1)

Optional Relationships   None

Attributes	✓	Which of the following attributes for each **Logical/Physical Data Store Cross-Reference Detail** does the software tool support?		
		Name	Description	Validation
DFM61A1		Logical Data Store ID	ID of Logical Data Store ID	ID of existing Data Store
DFM61A2		Physical Data Store IDs	IDs of Physical Data Store IDs	IDs of existing Data Store

83

Object Representation   None

Quality Criteria   None

Attribute Dependent Tests

Mandatory Relationships   None

Optional Relationships   None

Object Representation   None

Quality Criteria   None

DFM62 Process/Entity Matrix Entry

Each **Process/Entity Matrix Entry** has significance as cross-referencing an entity against a process. The values of the entry are as follows:

- 'u' (for "update") when a process updates an entity and/or,

- 'r' (for "read") when there is a flow from the main logical data store to the process or,

- null (a null entry) when the process does not access the entity. (1)

Mandatory Relationships	✓	Does the software tool ensure that each **Process/Entity Matrix Entry**
DFM62MR1		belongs to one and only one **Process/Entity Matrix**? (1)
DFM62MR2		contains one and only one **DFD Process**? (1)
DFM62MR3		contains one and only one **Entity Type**? (1)

Chapter 6
Data Flow Modelling

Optional Relationships   None

Attributes	✓	Which of the following attributes for each **Process/Entity Matrix Entry** does the software tool support?		
		Name	Description	Validation
DFM62A1		Process ID	ID of Process	ID of existing Process
DFM62A2		Entity ID	ID of Entity	ID of existing Entity
DFM62A3		Cell Value	Entry in cell	'u', and/or 'r' or null

Object Representation   None

Quality Criteria   None

Attribute Dependent Tests

Mandatory Relationships   None

Optional Relationships   None

Object Representation   None

Quality Criteria   None

7 Dialogue Design

This chapter contains tests for the following products and concepts:

Products

DDN1	Command Structure	88
DDN2	Dialogue Control Table	89
DDN3	Dialogue Element Descriptions	91
DDN4	Dialogue Level Help	92
DDN5	Dialogues	93
DDN6	Dialogue Structure	95
DDN7	Menu Structure	96
DDN8	Report Format	98
DDN9	Screen Format	99
DDN10	User Role/Function Matrix	100
DDN11	not used	
DDN12	User Roles	101

Concepts

DDN51	Dialogue	102
DDN52	Dialogue Structure Node	105
DDN53	Dialogue Element	112
DDN54	Logical Grouping of Dialogue Elements	114
DDN55	Menu	116
DDN56	Menu Structure Node	117
DDN57	Command Structure Option	122
DDN58	User Role	123
DDN59	User Role/Function Matrix Entry	124
DDN60	Logical Grouping of Dialogue Elements Description	126
DDN61	Dialogue Element Description	127

DDN1 Command Structure

Each **Command Structure** has significance as showing the directions that control can take when a user decides to complete or terminate a particular dialogue. This allows navigation to be implemented with or without menus. (3,5)

Mandatory Relationships	✓	Does the software tool ensure that each **Command Structure**
DDN1MR1		is associated with one and only one **Dialogue**? (5)
DDN1MR2		contains one or more **Command Structure Option**? (3,5)
DDN1MR3		belongs to one and only one **Logical Design**? (5)

Optional Relationships None

Attributes		✓	Which of the following attributes for each **Command Structure** does the software tool support?		
			Name	Description	Validation
DDN1A1			Name	Name of dialogue	Name of dialogue
DDN1A2			User Role	User of dialogue	Existing user role‡

Object Representation None

Quality Criteria None

Attribute Dependent Tests

Mandatory Relationships None

Chapter 7
Dialogue Design

Optional Relationships	None
Object Representation	None
Quality Criteria	None

DDN2 Dialogue Control Table

Each **Dialogue Control Table** has significance as identifying and capturing the navigation between the 'logical groupings of dialogue elements' under 'normal conditions'. This table also details the different order in which particular aspects of the dialogue may be undertaken. (5)

Mandatory Relationships	✓	Does the software tool ensure that each **Dialogue Control Table**
DDN2MR1		is for one and only one **Dialogue**? (5)
DDN2MR2		must describe the path through one or more **Logical Grouping of Dialogue Elements**? (5)

Testing Criteria for the SSADM
Version 4 Tools Conformance Scheme

Attributes	✓	Which of the following attributes for each **Dialogue Control Table** does the software tool support?		
		Name	Description	Validation
DDN2A1		Name	Name of dialogue	Existing dialogue
DDN2A2		LDGE (Repeating Group)		
		ID	ID of LDGE	Existing LDGE
		Min.	Minimum occurrence	Integer.
		Max.	Maximum occurrence	Integer.
		Ave.	Average occurrence	Integer.
		Default	Default pathway flag	'X'/null
		Alt. Paths	List of alternative pathways	'X'/null
DDN2A3		Default usage	Default %usage	Integer
DDN2A4		Alt. Paths usage	List of alternative pathways %usage	Integer

Object Representation   None

Quality Criteria	✓	Which of the following quality criteria does the software tool enforce?
DDN2QC1		Does the total of the percentage path usage (which is calculated for the default path and all alternative pathways within the dialogue) equal 100? (5)

Attribute Dependent Tests

Mandatory Relationships   None

Chapter 7
Dialogue Design

Optional Relationships   None

Object Representation   None

Quality Criteria   None

DDN3 Dialogue Element Descriptions

Each **Dialogue Element Descriptions** has significance as describing the elements of a dialogue. It provides the detailed documentation for a Dialogue Structure. (5)

Mandatory Relationships	✓	Does the software tool ensure that each **Dialogue Element Descriptions**
DDN3MR1		is for one and only one **Dialogue**? (5)
DDN3MR2		contains one or more **Logical Grouping of Dialogue Elements Description**? (5)
DDN3MR3		contains one or more **Dialogue Element Description**? (5)

Optional Relationships   None

Attributes	✓	Which of the following attributes for each **Dialogue Element Descriptions** does the software tool support?		
		Name	Description	Validation
DDN3A1		Name	Name of dialogue	Existing dialogue
DDN3A2		User Role	User role for dialogue	Existing user role‡
DDN3A3		Function	Function of dialogue	Existing function‡

Object Representation   None

Testing Criteria for the SSADM
Version 4 Tools Conformance Scheme

Quality Criteria	✓	Which of the following quality criteria does the software tool enforce?
DDN3QC1		Does every dialogue element include one or more data items? (5)

Attribute Dependent Tests

Mandatory Relationships   None

Optional Relationships   None

Object Representation   None

Quality Criteria   None

DDN4 Dialogue Level Help

Each **Dialogue Level Help** has significance as detailing the level of help the user (user role) requires to progress through this dialogue. (5)

Mandatory Relationships	✓	Does the software tool ensure that each **Dialogue Level Help**
DDN4MR1		must belong to one and only one **Dialogue**? (5)

Optional Relationships   None

Chapter 7
Dialogue Design

Attributes	✓	Which of the following attributes for each **Dialogue Level Help** does the software tool support?		
		Name	**Description**	**Validation**
DDN4A1		Dialogue Name	Name of dialogue	Unique
DDN4A2		User Role	User role for dialogue help	Existing user role
DDN4A3		Description	Record of dialogue level help	Text

Object Representation None

Quality Criteria None

Attribute Dependent Tests

Mandatory Relationships None

Optional Relationships None

Object Representation None

Quality Criteria None

DDN5 Dialogues

Each **Dialogues** has significance as packaging together details of all identified dialogues within the system. (5)

Mandatory Relationships	✓	Does the software tool ensure that each **Dialogues**
DDN5MR1		belongs to one and only one **Logical Process Model**? (5)
DDN5MR2		contains one or more **Dialogue**? (5)

Optional Relationships   None

Attributes	✓	Which of the following attributes for each **Dialogues** does the software tool support?		
		Name	**Description**	**Validation**
DDN5A1		Name	Name of set	Unique ID

Object Representation	✓	Does the software tool ensure that each **Dialogues** has the following object representation?
DDN5OB1		A **Dialogues** consists of a set of **Dialogue**

Quality Criteria	✓	Which of the following quality criteria does the software tool enforce?
DDN5QC1		Are all names within boxes on any Dialogue Structure cross-referenced to the corresponding Dialogue Element Descriptions? (5)
DDN5QC2		Are the logical grouping of dialogue elements (LGDE) within a Dialogue Structure composed of the same elements as the corresponding Dialogue Element Descriptions? (5)
DDN5QC3		Are all dialogue elements shown on a Dialogue Structure? (5)
DDN5QC4		Do all the dialogue elements in any dialogue appear in a Dialogue Element Descriptions? (5)
DDN5QC5		Are the LGDEs on each completed Dialogue Control Table consistent with its associated Dialogue Structure and Dialogue Element Descriptions? (5)

Attribute Dependent Tests

Mandatory Relationships   None

Chapter 7
Dialogue Design

Optional Relationships   None

Object Representation   None

Quality Criteria   None

DDN6 Dialogue Structure

Each **Dialogue Structure** has significance as a diagrammatic representation of a dialogue. Each leaf node on the Dialogue Structure equates to a dialogue element. Input / output operations are allocated to dialogue elements. (5)

Mandatory Relationships	✓	Does the software tool ensure that each **Dialogue Structure**
DDN6MR1		is for one and only one **Dialogue**? (5)
DDN6MR2		contains one or more **Dialogue Structure Node**? (5)

Optional Relationships   None

Attributes	✓	Which of the following attributes for each **Dialogue Structure** does the software tool support?		
		Name	Description	Validation
DDN6A1		Name	Name of diagram	Existing dialogue

Object Representation	✓	Does the software tool ensure that each **Dialogue Structure** has the following object representation?
DDN6OB1		A **Dialogue Structure** is composed of a set of **Dialogue Structure Node**

Testing Criteria for the SSADM
Version 4 Tools Conformance Scheme

Quality Criteria	✓	Which of the following quality criteria does the software tool enforce?
DDN6QC1		Does the dialogue name appear in the top box of the diagram? (5)
DDN6QC2		Is there only one root node? (5)
DDN6QC3		Have all dialogue elements been identified and assigned unique names? (5)

Attribute Dependent Tests

Mandatory Relationships   None

Optional Relationships   None

Object Representation   None

Quality Criteria   None

DDN7 Menu Structure

Each **Menu Structure** has significance as providing a diagrammatic representation of the menus to be used within the system. (3,5)

Mandatory Relationships	✓	Does the software tool ensure that each **Menu Structure**
DDN7MR1		describes one and only one **Menu**? (3,5)
DDN7MR2		is for one and only one **User Role**? (3)
DDN7MR3		contains one or more **Menu Structure Node**? (3,5)
DDN7MR4		belongs to one and only one **Logical Design**? (5)

Chapter 7
Dialogue Design

Optional Relationships   None

Attributes   ✓ Which of the following attributes for each **Menu Structure** does the software tool support?

	Name	Description	Validation
DDN7A1	Name	Name of diagram	Unique ID

Object Representation   ✓ Does the software tool ensure that each **Menu Structure** has the following object representation?

DDN7OB1	Each **Menu Structure** consists **Menu Structure Node**

Quality Criteria   ✓ Which of the following quality criteria does the software tool enforce?

DDN7QC1	Is the associated user role named in the top box? (3)

Attribute Dependent Tests

Mandatory Relationships   None

Optional Relationships   None

Object Representation   None

Quality Criteria   None

97

Testing Criteria for the SSADM
Version 4 Tools Conformance Scheme

DDN8 Report Format

Each **Report Format** has significance as showing the layout of a printed report as desired by the user. (3)

Mandatory Relationships   None

Optional Relationships   None

Attributes

✓	Which of the following attributes for each **Report Format** does the software tool support?		
DDN8A1	Name	Description	Validation
	Name	Name of report	Unique ID

Object Representation   None

Quality Criteria   None

Attribute Dependent Tests

Mandatory Relationships   None

Optional Relationships   None

Object Representation   None

Quality Criteria   None

Chapter 7
Dialogue Design

DDN9 Screen Format

Each **Screen Format** has significance as showing the layout that the user requires on the visual display unit screen. (3)

Mandatory Relationships   None

Optional Relationships   None

Attributes

✓	Which of the following attributes for each **Screen Format** does the software tool support?		
	Name	Description	Validation
DDN9A1	Name	Name of screen format	Unique ID
DDN9A2	Cross-reference	Cross-references to other products	Text documents
DDN9A3	Notes	Comments	Text

Object Representation   None

Quality Criteria   None

Attribute Dependent Tests

Mandatory Relationships   None

Optional Relationships   None

Object Representation   None

Quality Criteria   None

DDN10 User Role/Function Matrix

Each **User Role/Function Matrix** has significance as identifying dialogues by cross-referencing user roles and on-line functions (either enquiry or update). Reading down from the user roles axis also provides the (initial) Menu Structure for the system. (3)

Mandatory Relationships	✓	Does the software tool ensure that each **User Role/Function Matrix**
DDN10MR1		must belong to one and only one **Processing Specification**? (3)
DDN10MR2		must contain one or more **User Role/Function Matrix Entry**? (3)

Optional Relationships   None

Attributes		✓	Which of the following attributes for each **User Role / Function Matrix** does the software tool support?		
			Name	Description	Validation
DDN10A1			Name	Name of matrix	Unique ID

Object Representation	✓	Does the software tool ensure that each **User Role/Function Matrix** has the following object representation?
DDN10OB1		A **User Role/Function Matrix** consists of **User Role/Function Matrix Entry**

Quality Criteria	✓	Which of the following quality criteria does the software tool enforce?
DDN10QC1		Have all on-line functions been included in the matrix (as column headings)? (3)
DDN10QC2		Have all user roles been included in the matrix (as row headings)? (3)
DDN10QC3		Have all the necessary intersection points been identified? That is: - 'x' - dialogue - 'c' - critical dialogue - null - the user role does not make use of the function (3)

Attribute Dependent Tests

Mandatory Relationships None

Optional Relationships None

Object Representation None

Quality Criteria None

DDN12 User Roles

Each **User Roles** has significance as documenting the details for each user role identified as having a direct interest in the required system. (3)

Mandatory Relationships	✓	Does the software tool ensure that each **User Roles**
DDN12MR1		must contain one or more **User Role**? (3)

Optional Relationships None

Attributes

✓	Which of the following attributes for each **User Roles** does the software tool support?		
	Name	Description	Validation
DDN12A1	Identifier	ID of set	Unique ID

Object Representation None

Quality Criteria None

Attribute Dependent Tests

Mandatory Relationships None

Optional Relationships None

Object Representation None

Quality Criteria None

DDN51 Dialogue

Each **Dialogue** has significance as an object whose name serves to identify one way in which a particular on-line function is made available to users. A dialogue has one dialogue structure. (5)

Chapter 7
Dialogue Design

Mandatory Relationships	✓	Does the software tool ensure that each **Dialogue**
DDN51MR1		belongs to one and only one **Dialogues**? (5)
DDN51MR2		is described by one and only one **Dialogue Structure**? (5)
DDN51MR3		is associated with one or more **Command Structure** AND/OR has its access described by one or more **Menu Structure**? (5)
DDN51MR4		has its elements described by one and only one **Dialogue Element Descriptions**? (5)
DDN51MR5		is documented by one and only one **Dialogue Structure Node**? (5)
DDN51MR6		represents one or more **User Role / Function Matrix Entry**? (5)

Optional Relationships	✓	Does the software tool allow a **Dialogue**
DDN51OR1		to use one and only one **Dialogue Level Help**? (5)
DDN51OR2		to be referenced by one or more **Command Structure Option**? (5)
DDN51OR3		to be referenced by one or more **Menu Structure Node**? (5)
DDN51OR4		to be referenced by one or more **Function Definition**? (5)
DDN51OR5		to contain one and only one Command Structure? (5)

Attributes	✓	Which of the following attributes for each **Dialogue** does the software tool support?		
		Name	Description	Validation
DDN51A1		Name	Name of dialogue	Existing dialogue
DDN51A2		User Role	User role for dialogue	Existing user role
DDN51A3		Function	Function of dialogue	Existing function

Object Representation	✓	Does the software tool ensure that each **Dialogue** has the following object representation?
DDN51OB1		A **Dialogue** consists of • a Dialogue Structure • a Dialogue Element Descriptions • a Dialogue Control Table • a Dialogue Level Help

Quality Criteria   None

Attribute Dependent Tests

Mandatory Relationships   None

Optional Relationships   None

Object Representation   None

Quality Criteria   None

Chapter 7
Dialogue Design

DDN52 Dialogue Structure Node

Each **Dialogue Structure Node** has significance as a node on an Dialogue Structure. Each node must be one of the following types:

- a root node
- an intermediate node
- an elementary node.

Each node must have one of the following structures:

- a sequence node
- a selection node
- an iteration node
- a leaf node. (5)

Mandatory Relationships	✓	Does the software tool ensure that each **Dialogue Structure Node**
DDN52MR1		is part of one and only one **Dialogue Structure**? (5)

Optional Relationships	✓	Does the software tool allow a **Dialogue Structure Node**
DDN52OR1		to be the child of one and only one **Dialogue Structure Node**? (5)
DDN52OR2		to be the parent of one or more **Dialogue Structure Node**? (5)

105

Testing Criteria for the SSADM
Version 4 Tools Conformance Scheme

Attributes	✓	Which of the following attributes for each **Dialogue Structure Node** does the software tool support?		
		Name	Description	Validation
DDN52A1		Name	Name of node	Text
DDN52A2		Type	Type of node	ROOT/ INTERMEDIATE /ELEMENTARY
DDN52A3		Structure	Structure type of node	SEQUENCE/ SELECTION/ ITERATION/ LEAF

Object Representation   None

Quality Criteria   None

Attribute Dependent Tests

Where attribute: Type = "ROOT"

Mandatory Relationships	✓	Does the software tool ensure that each **Dialogue Structure Node**
DDN52ADMR1		is in one-to-one correspondence with one and only one **Dialogue**? (5)
DDN52ADMR2		is the parent of one or more **Dialogue Structure Node**? (5)

Chapter 7
Dialogue Design

Where attribute: Type = "INTERMEDIATE"

Mandatory Relationships	✓	Does the software tool ensure that each **Dialogue Structure Node**
DDN52ADMR3		is the child of one and only one **Dialogue Structure Node**? (5)
DDN52ADMR4		is the parent of one or more **Dialogue Structure Node**? (5)

Where attribute: Type = "ELEMENTARY"

Mandatory Relationships	✓	Does the software tool ensure that each **Dialogue Structure Node**
DDN52ADMR5		is the child of one and only one **Dialogue Structure Node**? (5)

Where attribute: Structure = "SEQUENCE"

Mandatory Relationships	✓	Does the software tool ensure that each **Dialogue Structure Node**
DDN52ADMR6		is the parent of two or more **Dialogue Structure Node**? (5)

Where attribute: Structure = "SELECTION"

Mandatory Relationships	✓	Does the software tool ensure that each **Dialogue Structure Node**
DDN52ADMR7		is the parent of two or more **Dialogue Structure Node**? (5)

Where attribute: Structure = "ITERATION"

Mandatory Relationships	✓	Does the software tool ensure that each **Dialogue Structure Node**
DDN52ADMR8		is the parent of one and only one **Dialogue Structure Node**? (5)

Where attribute: Structure = "LEAF"

Mandatory Relationships	✓	Does the software tool ensure that each **Dialogue Structure Node**
DDN52ADMR9		represents one and only one **Dialogue Element**? (5)

Optional Relationships   None

Where attribute: Type = "ROOT"

Object Representation	✓	Does the software tool ensure that each **Dialogue Structure Node** has the following object representation for the given attribute value?
DDN52ADOB1		Dialogue Name

Chapter 7
Dialogue Design

Where attribute: Structure = "SEQUENCE"

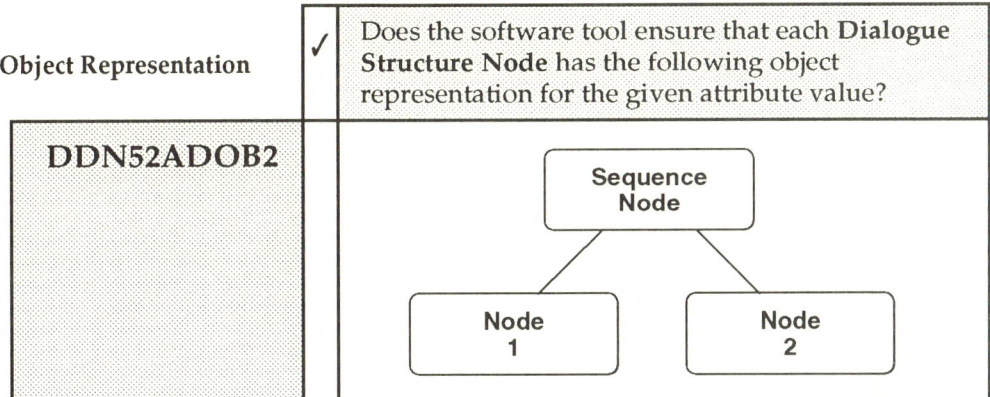

Where attribute: Structure = "SELECTION"

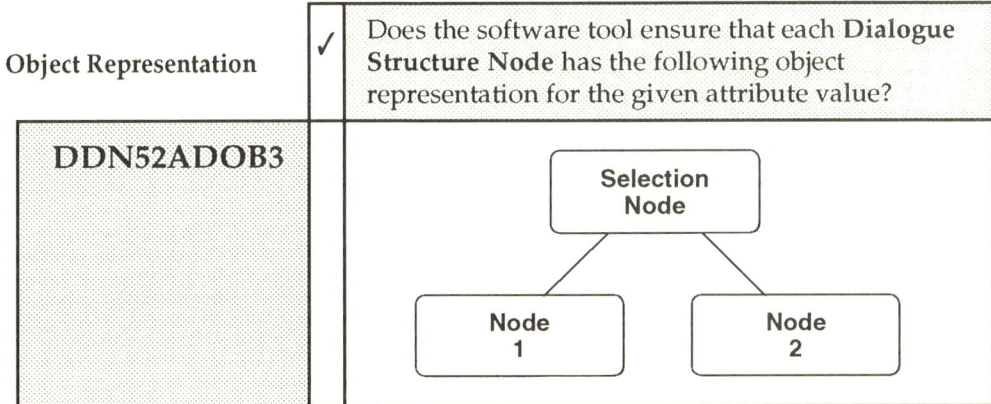

Where attribute: Structure = "ITERATION"

Object Representation	✓	Does the software tool ensure that each **Dialogue Structure Node** has the following object representation for the given attribute value?
DDN52ADOB4		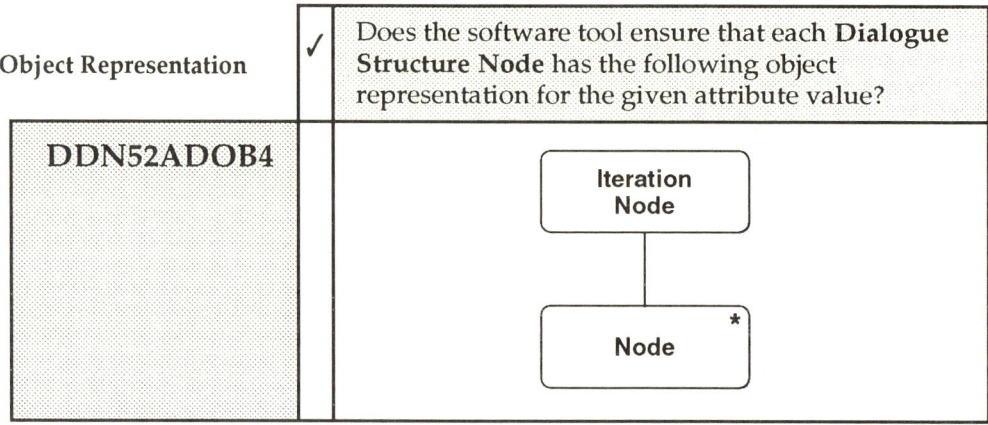

Where attribute: Structure = "LEAF"

Object Representation	✓	Does the software tool ensure that each **Dialogue Structure Node** has the following object representation for the given attribute value?
DDN52ADOB5		Dialogue Element Name

Where attribute: Type = "ROOT"

Quality Criteria	✓	Which of the following quality criteria does the software tool enforce?
DDN52ADQC1		Attribute: Name = An existing Dialogue Name

Where attribute: Type = "ELEMENTARY"

Quality Criteria	✓	Which of the following quality criteria does the software tool enforce?
DDN52ADQC2		Attribute: Structure = "LEAF"

Where attribute: Structure = "ITERATION"

Quality Criteria	✓	Which of the following quality criteria does the software tool enforce?
DDN52ADQC3		Attribute: Type = "INTERMEDIATE"

Where attribute: Structure = "LEAF"

Quality Criteria	✓	Which of the following quality criteria does the software tool enforce?
DDN52ADQC4		Attribute: Type = "ELEMENTARY" Attribute: Name = An existing Dialogue Element Name The Dialogue Structure Node must have no children

Testing Criteria for the SSADM
Version 4 Tools Conformance Scheme

DDN53 Dialogue Element

Each **Dialogue Element** has significance as a section of an input or output data flow which may consist of many data items. Each Dialogue Element is represented as a box on a Dialogue Structure (5)

Mandatory Relationships	✓	Does the software tool ensure that each **Dialogue Element**
DDN53MR1		is part of one and only one **Logical Grouping of Dialogue Elements**? (5)
DDN53MR2		is documented by one and only one **Dialogue Structure Node**? (5)
DDN53MR3		is documented by one and only one **Dialogue Element Description**? (5)

Optional Relationships   None

Attributes	✓	Which of the following attributes for each **Dialogue Element** does the software tool support?	
		Name	Description	Validation
DDN53A1		Name	Name of element	Unique ID

Chapter 7
Dialogue Design

Object Representation	✓	Does the software tool ensure that each **Dialogue Element** has the following object representation?
DDN53OB1		Dialogue Element Name OR Dialogue Element Name (input) OR Dialogue Element Name (output)

Quality Criteria   None

Attribute Dependent Tests

Mandatory Relationships   None

Optional Relationships   None

Object Representation   None

Quality Criteria   None

113

Testing Criteria for the SSADM
Version 4 Tools Conformance Scheme

DDN54 Logical Grouping of Dialogue Elements

Each **Logical Grouping of Dialogue Elements** has significance as a substructure of a complete dialogue structure. (5)

Mandatory Relationships ✓ Does the software tool ensure that each **Logical Grouping of Dialogue Elements**

DDN54MR1	is documented by one and only one **Logical Grouping of Dialogue Elements Description**? (5)
DDN54MR2	must have its path described by one and only one **Dialogue Control Table**? (5)
DDN54MR3	must contain one or more **Dialogue Element**? (5)

Optional Relationships   None

Attributes ✓ Which of the following attributes for each **Logical Grouping of Dialogue Elements** does the software tool support?

	Name	Description	Validation
DDN54A1	Name	Name of LDGE	Unique ID
DDN54A2	Elements	List of dialogue elements	Existing dialogue elements
DDN54A3	Optionality	Optionality of LDGE	'M' / 'O' / 'M/O'

Chapter 7
Dialogue Design

Object Representation	✓	Does the software tool ensure that each **Logical Grouping of Dialogue Elements** has the following object representation?
DDN54OB1		*[Diagram: Dialogue Name tree with Sequence Node (Dialogue Element 1 (input), Dialogue Element 2 (output)) labeled LGDE-1; Selection Node (Dialogue Element 3 (input), ...) labeled LGDE-2; Iteration Node (Node* with Dialogue Element 1 (input), Dialogue Element 4 (output)) labeled LGDE-3]*

Quality Criteria	✓	Which of the following quality criteria does the software tool enforce?
DDN54QC1		Does the LGDE consist of one or more dialogue elements and their components? (5)

Attribute Dependent Tests

Mandatory Relationships   None

Optional Relationships   None

Object Representation   None

Quality Criteria   None

Testing Criteria for the SSADM
Version 4 Tools Conformance Scheme

DDN55 Menu

Each **Menu** has significance as an object whose name serves to identify a combination of options (either dialogues and / or other menus which may be made available to users). (3,5)

Mandatory Relationships	✓	Does the software tool ensure that each **Menu**
DDN55MR1		is described by one and only one **Menu Structure**? (3,5)
DDN55MR2		is documented by one and only one **Menu Structure Node**? (3,5)

Optional Relationships	✓	Does the software tool allow a **Menu**
DDN55OR1		to be referenced by one or more **Command Structure Option**? (3,5)
DDN55OR2		to be referenced by one or more **Menu Structure Node**? (3,5)

Attributes	✓	Which of the following attributes for each **Menu** does the software tool support?		
		Name	Description	Validation
DDN55A1		Name	Name of Menu	Unique ID

Object Representation	✓	Does the software tool ensure that each **Menu** has the following object representation?
DDN55OB1		Main Menu Name (MEN01) → Dialogue Name (DIAL01), Sub-Menu Name (MEN02) → Dialogue Name (DIAL03), Dialogue Name (DIAL04); Dialogue Name (DIAL02)

Quality Criteria   None

Attribute Dependent Tests

Mandatory Relationships   None

Optional Relationships   None

Object Representation   None

Quality Criteria   None

DDN56 Menu Structure Node

Each **Menu Structure Node** has significance as a node on a Menu Structure. Each node must be one of the following types:

- a root node
- an intermediate node
- an elementary node

Each node must have one of the following structures:

- a dialogue node
- a menu node. (3,5)

Mandatory Relationships	✓	Does the software tool ensure that each **Menu Structure Node**
DDN56MR1		is part of one and only one **Menu Structure**? (3,5)

Testing Criteria for the SSADM
Version 4 Tools Conformance Scheme

Optional Relationships	✓	Does the software tool allow a **Menu Structure Node**		
DDN56OR1		to be the child of one and only one **Menu Structure Node**? (3,5)		
DDN56OR2		to be the parent of one or more **Menu Structure Node**? (3,5)		

Attributes	✓	Which of the following attributes for each **Menu Structure Node** does the software tool support?		
		Name	Description	Validation
DDN56A1		Name	Name of node	Text
DDN56A2		Type	Type of node	ROOT/ INTERMEDIATE /ELEMENTARY
DDN56A3		Structure	Structure type of node	DIALOGUE/ MENU

Object Representation   None

Quality Criteria   None

Attribute Dependent Tests

Where attribute: Type = "ROOT"

Mandatory Relationships	✓	Does the software tool ensure that each **Menu Structure Node**
DDN56ADMR1		is in one-to-one correspondence with one and only one **Menu**? (3,5)
DDN56ADMR2		is the parent of one or more **Menu Structure Node**? (3,5)

Chapter 7
Dialogue Design

Where attribute: Type = "INTERMEDIATE"

Mandatory Relationships	✓	Does the software tool ensure that each **Menu Structure Node**
DDN56ADMR3		is the child of one and only one **MenuStructure Node**? (3,5)
DDN56ADMR4		is the parent of one or more **Menu Structure Node**? (3,5)

Where attribute: Type = "ELEMENTARY"

Mandatory Relationships	✓	Does the software tool ensure that each **Menu Structure Node**
DDN56ADMR5		is the child of one and only one **Menu Structure Node**? (3,5)

Where attribute: Structure = "DIALOGUE"

Mandatory Relationships	✓	Does the software tool ensure that each **Menu Structure Node**
DDN56ADMR6		represents one and only one **Dialogue**? (3,5)

Where attribute: Structure = "MENU"

Mandatory Relationships	✓	Does the software tool ensure that each **Menu Structure Node**
DDN56ADMR7		represents one and only one **Menu**? (3,5)

Where attribute: Type = "ROOT"

Object Representation	✓	Does the software tool ensure that each **Menu Structure Node** has the following object representation?
DDN56ADOB1		Main Menu Name MEN01

Where attribute: Type = "DIALOGUE"

Object Representation	✓	Does the software tool ensure that each **Menu Structure Node** has the following object representation?
DDN56ADOB2		Dialogue Name DIAL01

Where attribute: Type = "MENU"

Object Representation	✓	Does the software tool ensure that each **Menu Structure Node** has the following object representation?
DDN56ADOB3		Sub-Menu Name MEN02

Chapter 7
Dialogue Design

Where attribute: Type = "ROOT"

Quality Criteria	✓	Which of the following quality criteria does the software tool enforce?
DDN56ADQC1		Attribute: Structure = "MENU" (3,5) Attribute: Name = An Existing Menu Name

Where attribute: Structure = "DIALOGUE"

Quality Criteria	✓	Which of the following quality criteria does the software tool enforce?
DDN56ADQC2		Attribute: Type = "ELEMENTARY" (3,5)

Where attribute: Structure = "MENU"

Quality Criteria	✓	Which of the following quality criteria does the software tool enforce?
DDN56ADQC3		Attribute: Type = "INTERMEDIATE" (3,5)

Where attribute: Type = "ELEMENTARY"

Quality Criteria	✓	Which of the following quality criteria does the software tool enforce?
DDN56ADQC4		The Menu Structure Node has no children (3,5)

Testing Criteria for the SSADM
Version 4 Tools Conformance Scheme

DDN57 Command Structure Option

Each **Command Structure Option** has significance as a reference to a menu of a dialogue that can be invoked

Mandatory Relationships	✓	Does the software tool ensure that each **Command Structure Option**
DDN57MR1		is part of one and only one **Command Structure**? (3,5)
DDN57MR2		refences one and only one **Dialogue** (5) OR references one and only one **Menu**? (3,5)

Optional Relationships   None

Attributes	✓	Which of the following attributes for each **Command Structure Node** does the software tool support?		
		Name	Description	Validation
DDN57A1		Identifier	ID of option	Unique
DDN57A2		Option	Description of option	Text
DDN57A3		Path	Path of option	Menu/Dialogue
DDN57A4		Name	Name of menu /dialogue	Existing menu /dialogue

Object Representation   None

Quality Criteria   None

Attribute Dependent Tests

Mandatory Relationships   None

Optional Relationships   None

Chapter 7
Dialogue Design

Object Representation   None

Quality Criteria   None

DDN58 User Role

Each **User Role** has significance as a grouping of activities common to a collection of users. (3)

Mandatory Relationships	✓	Does the software tool ensure that each **User Role**
DDN58MR1		must belong to one and only one **User Roles**? (3)
DDN58MR2		must have its options described by one and only one **Menu Structure**? (3)
DDN58MR3		is referenced by one or more **User Role / Function Matrix Entry**? (3)

Optional Relationships	✓	Does the software tool allow a **User Role**
DDN58OR1		to be referenced by one or more **Function Definition**? (3)
DDN58OR2		to be referenced by one or more **Attribute/Data Item Description**? (3)
DDN58OR3		to be referenced by one or more **Entity Description**? (3)
DDN58OR4		to be referenced by one or more **Grouped Domain Description**? (3)
DDN58OR5		to be referenced by one or more **Relationship Description**? (3)
DDN58OR6		to be the subject of one or more **Prototype Pathway**? (3)
DDN58OR7		to be detailed by one or more **User Catalogue Entry**? (3)

Testing Criteria for the SSADM
Version 4 Tools Conformance Scheme

Attributes	✓	Which of the following attributes for each **User Role** does the software tool support?		
		Name	**Description**	**Validation**
DDN58A1 **DDN58A2**		Name	Name/ID of role	Unique ID
		Job Details (Repeating Group) Activities	Job title	Text
		Title	Multiple role activities	Text

Object Representation   None

Quality Criteria   None

Attribute Dependent Tests

Mandatory Relationships   None

Optional Relationships   None

Object Representation   None

Quality Criteria   None

DDN59 User Role/Function Matrix Entry

Each **User Role/Function Matrix Entry** has significance as mapping the correspondence between a user role and an on-line function. (3)

Chapter 7
Dialogue Design

Mandatory Relationships	✓	Does the software tool ensure that each **User Role/Function Matrix Entry**		
DDN59MR1		belongs to one and only one **User Role/Function Matrix**? (3)		
DDN59MR2		references one and only one **User Role**? (3)		
DDN59MR3		references one and only one **Function**? (3)		

Optional Relationships	✓	Does the software tool allow a **User Role / Function Matrix Entry**		
DDN59OR1		to be represented by one and only one **Dialogue**? (3)		

Attributes	✓	Which of the following attributes for each **User Role / Function Matrix Entry** does the software tool support?		
		Name	Description	Validation
DDN59A1		User Role	Name of user role	Existing user role
DDN59A2		Function	Name of function	Existing function
DDN59A3		Value	Value of cell	'x'/'c'/null

Object Representation   None

Quality Criteria   None

Attribute Dependent Tests

Mandatory Relationships   None

Optional Relationships   None

Object Representation   None

125

Quality Criteria   None

DDN60 Logical Grouping of Dialogue Elements Description

Each **Logical Grouping of Elements Description** has significance as a Logical Grouping of Dialogue Elements. (5)

Mandatory Relationships	✓	Does the software tool ensure that each **Logical Grouping of Dialogue Elements Description**
DDN60MR1		is part of one and only one **Dialogue Element Description**? (5)
DDN60MR2		has its path described by one and only one **Dialogue Control Table**? (5)
DDN60MR3		contains one or more **Dialogue Element Descriptions**? (5)
DDN60MR4		documents one and only one **Logical Grouping of Dialogue Elements**? (5)

Optional Relationships   None

Attributes	✓	Which of the following attributes for each **Logical Grouping of Dialogue Elements Description** does the software tool support?		
		Name	Description	Validation
DDN60A1		Name	Name of LDGE	Unique ID
DDN60A2		Elements	List of dialogue elements	Existing dialogue elements
DDN60A3		Optionality	Optionality of LDGE	'M' / 'O' / 'M/O'

Object Representation   None

Chapter 7
Dialogue Design

Quality Criteria   None

Attribute Dependent Tests

Mandatory Relationships   None

Optional Relationships   none

Object Representation   None

Quality Criteria   None

DDN61 Dialogue Element Description

Each Dialogue Element Description has significance as a description of a Dialogue Element. (5)

Mandatory Relationships	✓	Does the software tool ensure that each **Dialogue Element Description**
DDN61MR1		contains one or more **Attribute Type**? (5)
DDN61MR2		is part of one and only one **Logical Grouping of Dialogue Elements Description**? (5)
DDN61MR3		is documented by one and only one **Dialogue Structure Node**? (5)

Optional Relationships   None

127

Testing Criteria for the SSADM
Version 4 Tools Conformance Scheme

Attributes	✓	Which of the following attributes for each **Dialogue Element Description** does the software tool support?		
		Name	Description	Validation
DDN61A1		Name	Name of element	Unique ID
DDN61A2		Data Items	List of Data Items	Existing Attribute Types

Object Representation   None

Quality Criteria   None

Attribute Dependent Tests

Mandatory Relationships   None

Optional Relationships   none

Object Representation   None

Quality Criteria   None

Chapter 8
Entity Event Modelling

8 Entity Event Modelling

This chapter contains tests for the following products and concepts:

Products

EEM1	Effect Correspondence Diagram	130
EEM2	Entity Life History	132
EEM3	Event/Entity Matrix	133

Concepts

EEM51	Event	135
EEM52	Effect	136
EEM53	ELH Node	136
EEM54	ECD Node	147
EEM55	Effect Qualifier	152
EEM56	Effect Correspondence	153
EEM57	Entity Role	155
EEM58	ELH Operation	156
EEM59	Pre/Post State Indicator Value	158
EEM60	ELH Structure	160
EEM61	Event/Entity Matrix Entry	163

Testing Criteria for the SSADM
Version 4 Tools Conformance Scheme

EEM1 Effect Correspondence Diagram

Each **Effect Correspondence Diagram** has significance as showing the different effects of an event on data within the system and how those effects are inter-related. (3,5)

Mandatory Relationships	✓	Does the software tool ensure that each **Effect Correspondence Diagram**
EEM1MR1		belongs to one and only one **Logical Process Model**? (5)
EEM1MR2		belongs to one and only one **Processing Specification**? (3)
EEM1MR3		is the basis for one and only one **Update Process Model**? (5)
EEM1MR4		describes one and only one **Event**? (3)
EEM1MR5		contains one or more **ECD Node**? (3)
EEM1MR6		receives input frome one or more **Attribute Type**? (3)

Optional Relationships	✓	Does the software tool allow an **Effect Correspondence Diagram**
EEM1OR1		to contain one or more **Effect Correspondence**? (3)

Attributes		✓	Which of the following attributes for each **Effect Correspondence Diagram** does the software tool support?		
			Name	Description	Validation
EEM1A1			Name	Name of diagram	Name of existing event
EEM1A2			Event data	List of attributes input into the update processing	Existing attribute types

Chapter 8
Entity Event Modelling

Object Representation	✓	Does the software tool ensure that each **Effect Correspondence Diagram** has the following object representation? (3)
EEM1OB1		An **Effect Correspondence Diagram** is composed of • ECD Node • Effect Correspondence • EVENT DATA (List of attributes)

Quality Criteria	✓	Which of the following quality criteria does the software tool enforce?
EEM1QC1		Have all the entities which are affected by one event been documented on the same Effect Correspondence Diagram? (3)
EEM1QC2		Is each Effect Correspondence Diagram for a different event? (3)

Attribute Dependent Tests

Mandatory Relationships   None

Optional Relationships   None

Object Representation   None

Quality Criteria   None

Testing Criteria for the SSADM
Version 4 Tools Conformance Scheme

EEM2 Entity Life History

Each **Entity Life History** has significance as a sequential structure of nodes that identify all the events that can affect an entity. The Entity Life History is a combination of all possible lives for every entity of the entity type. (3) (5)

Mandatory Relationships	✓	Does the software tool ensure that each **Entity Life History**
EEM2MR1		belongs to one and only one **Processing Specification**? (3)
EEM2MR2		is the basis for one or more **Update Process Model**? (5)
EEM2MR3		describes one and only one **Entity Type**? (3)
EEM2MR4		contains one or more **ELH Structure**? (3)

Optional Relationships   None

Attributes	✓	Which of the following attributes for each **Entity Life History** does the software tool support?	
		Name	Description	Validation
EEM2A1		Name	Name of diagram	Name of existing entity

Object Representation	✓	Does the software tool ensure that each **Entity Life History** has the following object representation?
EEM2OB1		An **Entity Life History** is composed of • **ENTITY** • **ELH Structure** • **Pre/Post State Indicator Value**

Chapter 8
Entity Event Modelling

Quality Criteria	✓	Which of the following quality criteria does the software tool enforce?
EEM2QC1		Does the entity name appear in the top box of the diagram? (3)
EEM2QC2		Is there only one root node? (3)
EEM2QC3		Have all State Indicator Values been included as appropriate? (5)

Attribute Dependent Tests

Mandatory Relationships None

Optional Relationships None

Object Representation None

Quality Criteria None

EEM3 Event/Entity Matrix

Each **Event/Entity Matrix** has significance as a grid that is used to identify which entities are affected by a particular event. (3)

Mandatory Relationships	✓	Does the software tool ensure that each **Event/Entity Matrix**
EEM3MR1		contains one or more **Event/Entity Matrix Entry**? (3)

Optional Relationships None

133

Testing Criteria for the SSADM
Version 4 Tools Conformance Scheme

Attributes	✓	Which of the following attributes for each **Event/ Entity Matrix** does the software tool support?		
		Name	Description	Validation
EEM3A1		Name	Name of Matrix	Text

Object Representation   None

Quality Criteria	✓	Which of the following quality criteria does the software tool enforce?
EEM3QC1		Are all entities from the LDM listed? (3)
EEM3QC2		Is there any event with no corresponding entity to act on it? (3)

Attribute Dependent Tests

Mandatory Relationships   None

Optional Relationships   None

Object Representation   None

Quality Criteria   None

Chapter 8
Entity Event Modelling

EEM51 Event

Each **Event** has significance as triggering a process. An event is identified by its Event Name. A single event may cause the state of more than one entity to change. (3)

Mandatory Relationships	✓	Does the software tool ensure that each **Event**
EEM51MR1		is described by one and only one **Effect Correspondence Diagram**? (3)
EEM51MR2		causes one or more **Effect**? (3)

Optional Relationships	✓	Does the software tool allow an **Event**
EEM51OR1		to be referenced by one or more **Event/Entity Matrix Entry**? (3)
EEM51OR2		to be documented by one or more **ELH Structure**? (3)
EEM51OR3		to be referenced by one or more **Function Definition**? (3)

Attributes	✓	Which of the following attributes for each **Event/Entity Matrix** does the software tool support?		
		Name	Description	Validation
EEM51A1		Name	Name of Event	Unique ID

Object Representation   None

Quality Criteria   None

Attribute Dependent Tests

Mandatory Relationships None

135

Testing Criteria for the SSADM
Version 4 Tools Conformance Scheme

Optional Relationships   None

Object Representation   None

Quality Criteria   None

EEM52 Effect

Each **Effect** has significance as the change to the state of a single entity by a single event. (3, 5)

Mandatory Relationships	✓	Does the software tool ensure that each **Effect**
EEM52MR1		is triggered by one and only one **Event**? (3)
EEM52MR2		is represented by one or more **ELH Node**? (3)
EEM52MR3		is represented by one and only one **ECD Node**? (3)
EEM52MR4		has one or more **Pre/Post State Indicator Value**? (5)

Optional Relationships	✓	Does the software tool allow an **Effect**
EEM52OR1		to be further qualified by one or more **Entity Role**? (3)
EEM52OR2		to be further qualified by one or more **Effect Qualifier**? (3)
EEM52OR3		to be composed of one or more **ELH Operation**? (3)

Attributes		✓	Which of the following attributes for each **Effect** does the software tool support?		
			Name	Description	Validation
	EEM52A1		Identifier	Name of Event + Name of Entity	Name of existing event and entity

Chapter 8
Entity Event Modelling

Object Representation	✓	Does the software tool ensure that each **Effect** has the following object representation? (3)
EEM52OB1		See **ELH Node** See **ECD Node**

Quality Criteria   None

Attribute Dependent Tests

Mandatory Relationships   None

Optional Relationships   None

Object Representation   None

Quality Criteria   None

EEM53 ELH Node

Each **ELH Node** has significance as a node on an Entity Life History. Each node must be one of the following types:

- a root node
- an intermediate node
- an elementary node

Each node must have one of the following structures:

- a sequence node
- a selection node
- an iteration node
- a parallel structure node
- an effect node
- an operation node. (3, 5)

137

Testing Criteria for the SSADM
Version 4 Tools Conformance Scheme

Mandatory Relationships	✓	Does the software tool ensure that each **ELH Node**	
EEM53MR1		is part of one and only one **ELH Structure**? (3)	

Optional Relationships	✓	Does the software tool allow an **ELH Node**	
EEM53OR1		to be the child of one and only one **ELH Node**? (3)	
EEM53OR2		to be the parent of one or more **ELH Node**? (3)	

Attributes		✓	Which of the following attributes for each **ELH Node** does the software tool support?		
			Name	**Description**	**Validation**
	EEM53A1		Name	Name of node	Text
	EEM53A2		Type	Type of node	ROOT/ INTERMEDIATE /ELEMENTARY
	EEM53A3		Structure	Structure type of node	SEQUENCE/ SELECTION/ ITERATION/ PARALLEL/ EFFECT/ OPERATION/ NULL-EVENT
	EEM53A4		Quit	Quit flag for ELH Node	'Q' + Cardinal /null
	EEM53A5		Resumes	List of Resume flags for ELH Node	'R' + Cardinal /null

Object Representation   None

Chapter 8
Entity Event Modelling

Quality Criteria   None

Attribute Dependent Tests

Where Attribute: Type = "ROOT"

Mandatory Relationships	✓	Does the software tool ensure that each ELH Node
EEM53ADMR1		is in one-to-one correspondence with one and only one **Entity Type**? (3)
EEM53ADMR2		is the parent of *two* or more **ELH Node**? (3)

Where Attribute: Type = "INTERMEDIATE"

Mandatory Relationships	✓	Does the software tool ensure that each ELH Node
EEM53ADMR3		is the child of one and only one **ELH Node**? (3)
EEM53ADMR4		is the parent of one or more **ELH Node**? (3)

Where Attribute: Type = "ELEMENTARY"

Mandatory Relationships	✓	Does the software tool ensure that each ELH Node
EEM53ADMR5		is the child of one and only one **ELH Node**? (3)

Where Attribute: Structure = "SEQUENCE"

Mandatory Relationships	✓	Does the software tool ensure that each ELH Node
EEM53ADMR6		is the parent of *two* or more **ELH Node**? (3)

Where Attribute: Structure = "SELECTION"

Mandatory Relationships	✓	Does the software tool ensure that each **ELH Node**
EEM53ADMR7		is the parent of *two* or more **ELH Node**? (3)

Where Attribute: Structure = "ITERATION"

Mandatory Relationships	✓	Does the software tool ensure that each **ELH Node**
EEM53ADMR8		is the parent of one and only one **ELH Node**? (3)

Where Attribute: Structure = "PARALLEL"

Mandatory Relationships	✓	Does the software tool ensure that each **ELH Node**
EEM53ADMR9		is the parent of *two* or more **ELH Node**? (3)

Where Attribute: Structure = "EFFECT"

Mandatory Relationships	✓	Does the software tool ensure that each **ELH Node**
EEM53ADMR10		represents one and only one **Effect**? (3)
EEM53ADMR11		must document one or more **Pre/Post State Indicator Value**? (5)

Where Attribute: Structure = "OPERATION"

Mandatory Relationships	✓	Does the software tool ensure that each **ELH Node**
EEM53ADMR12		must represent one and only one **ELH Operation**? (3)

Chapter 8
Entity Event Modelling

Where Attribute: Structure = "NULL-EVENT"

Mandatory Relationships	✓	Does the software tool ensure that each **ELH Node**
EEM53ADMR13		is the child of one and only one **ELH Node**? (3)

Optional Relationships   None

Where Attribute: Type = "ROOT"

Object Representation	✓	Does the software tool ensure that each **ELH Node** has the following object representation for the given attribute value?
EEM53ADOB1		Entity Name

Where Attribute: Structure = "SEQUENCE"

Object Representation	✓	Does the software tool ensure that each **ELH Node** has the following object representation for the given attribute value?
EEM53ADOB2		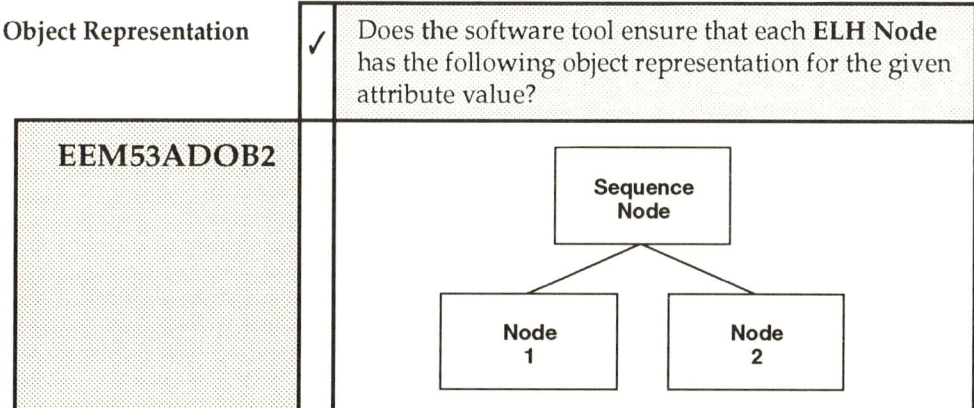

141

Testing Criteria for the SSADM Version 4 Tools Conformance Scheme

Where Attribute: Structure = "SELECTION"

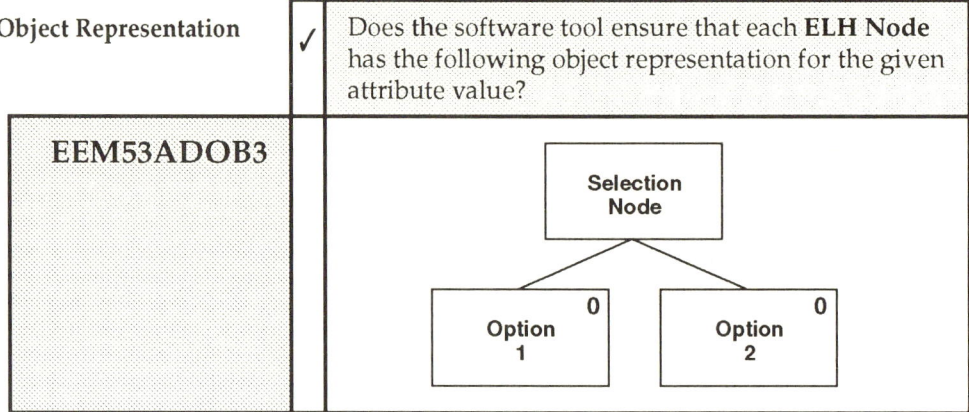

Where Attribute: Structure = "ITERATION"

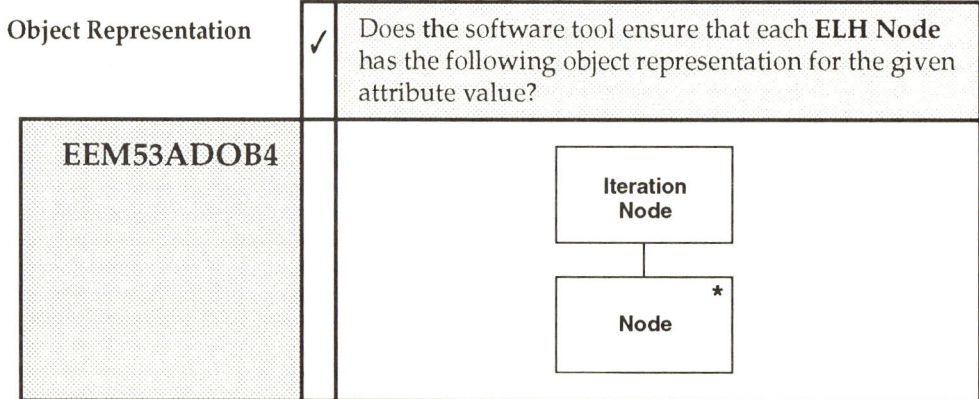

Chapter 8
Entity Event Modelling

Where Attribute: Structure = "PARALLEL"

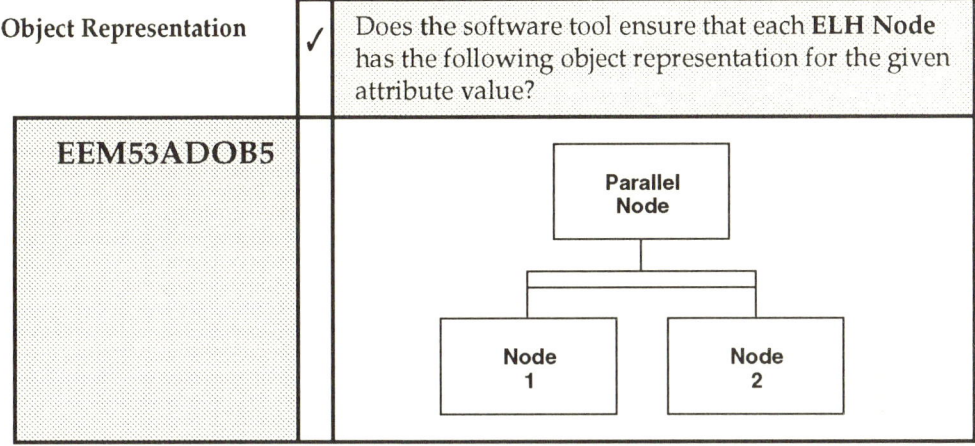

Where Attribute: Structure = "EFFECT"

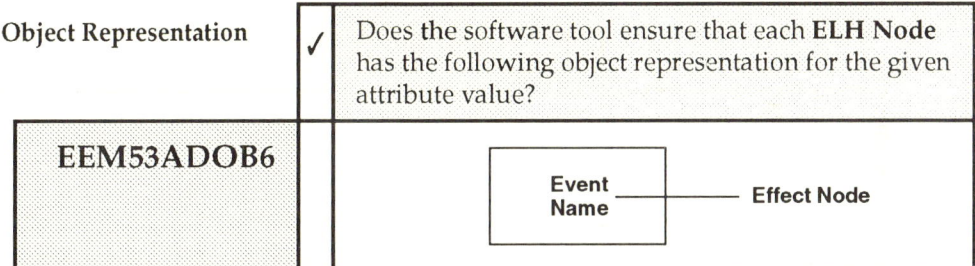

Where Attribute: Structure = "OPERATION"

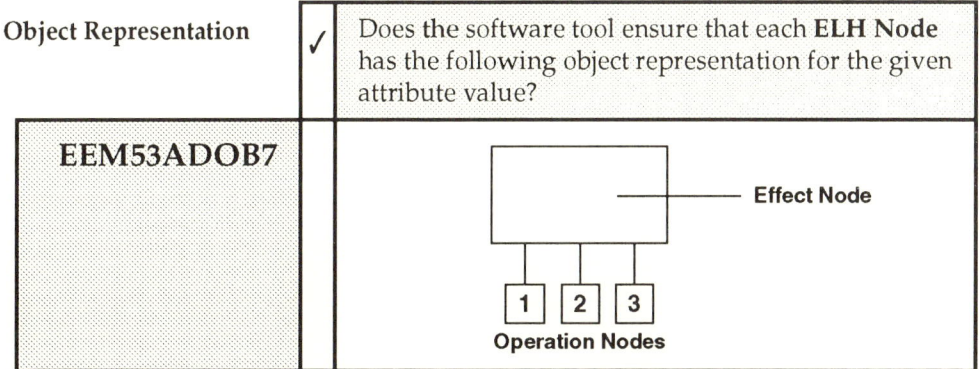

143

Where Attribute: Structure = "NULL-EVENT"

Object Representation	✓	Does the software tool ensure that each **ELH Node** has the following object representation for the given attribute value?
EEM53ADOB8		–

Where Attribute: Quit = "Qn" where n is any Cardinal

Object Representation	✓	Does the software tool ensure that each **ELH Node** has the following object representation for the given attribute value?
EEM53ADOB9		Q1 Event Name

Where Attribute: Quit = "Rn" where n is any Cardinal

Object Representation	✓	Does the software tool ensure that each **ELH Node** has the following object representation for the given attribute value?
EEM53ADOB10		R1 Event Name

Where Attribute: Type = "ROOT"

Quality Criteria	✓	Which of the following quality criteria does the software tool enforce?
EEM53ADQC1		Attribute: Name = An existing Entity Type Name (3)

Where Attribute: Type = "ELEMENTARY"

Quality Criteria	✓	Which of the following quality criteria does the software tool enforce?
EEM53ADQC2		Attribute: Structure = "EFFECT" or "OPERATION" (3)

Where Attribute: Type = "ITERATION"

Quality Criteria	✓	Which of the following quality criteria does the software tool enforce?
EEM53ADQC3		Attribute: Type = "INTERMEDIATE" (3)

Where Attribute: Type = "PARALLEL"

Quality Criteria	✓	Which of the following quality criteria does the software tool enforce?
EEM53ADQC4		Attribute: Type = "INTERMEDIATE" (3)

Where Attribute: Type = "EFFECT"

Quality Criteria	✓	Which of the following quality criteria does the software tool enforce?
EEM53ADQC5		Attribute: Name = An existing Event Name (3)
EEM53ADQC6		Attribute: Type = "INTERMEDIATE" or "ELEMENTARY" (3)
EEM53ADQC7		Children ELH NODEs: Attribute: Structure = "OPERATION" (3)

Where Attribute: Type = "OPERATION"

Quality Criteria	✓	Which of the following quality criteria does the software tool enforce?
EEM53ADQC8		Attribute: Name = A Cardinal (3)
EEM53ADQC9		Attribute: Type = "ELEMENTARY" (3)
EEM53ADQC10		Parent ELH NODEs: Attribute: Structure = "EFFECT" (3)
EEM53ADQC11		The ELH NODE must have no children (3)

Where Attribute: Type = "NULL-EVENT"

Quality Criteria	✓	Which of the following quality criteria does the software tool enforce?
EEM53ADQC12		Attribute: Type = "ELEMENTARY" (3)
EEM53ADQC13		Attribute: Name = "-" (3)
EEM53ADQC14		The ELH NODE must have no children (3)

Where Attribute: Quit = "Qn" where n is any Cardinal

Quality Criteria	✓	Which of the following quality criteria does the software tool enforce?
EEM53ADQC15		There must be one and only one other effect with Resume = 'Rn' (3)

Where Attribute: Resume = "Rn" where n is any Cardinal

Quality Criteria	✓	Which of the following quality criteria does the software tool enforce?
EEM53ADQC16		There must be one or more other effects with Quit = 'Qn' (3)

Chapter 8
Entity Event Modelling

EEM54 ECD Node

Each **ECD Node** has significance as a node on an Effect Correspondence Diagram. Each node must be one of the following types:

- a composite node
- an elementary node (3)

Each node must have one of the following structures:

- an effect node
- a selection node
- an iteration node.

Mandatory Relationships	✓	Does the software tool ensure that each **ECD Node**
EEM54MR1		is part of one and only one **Effect Correspondence Diagram**? (3)

Optional Relationships	✓	Does the software tool allow an **ECD Node**
EEM54OR1		to be sourced by one or more **Effect Correspondence**? (3)
EEM54OR2		to be targeted by one or more **Effect Correspondence**? (3)

Testing Criteria for the SSADM
Version 4 Tools Conformance Scheme

Attributes	✓	Which of the following attributes for each ECD Node does the software tool support?		
		Name	Description	Validation
EEM54A1		Name	Name of node	<Entity>/ <Entity> + <Effect Qualifier> and/or <Entity Role> / A SET OF<Entity>
EEM54A2		Type	Type of node	COMPOSITE/ ELEMENTARY
EEM54A3		Structure	Structure type of node	EFFECT/ SELECTION/ ITERATION
EEM54A4		Simultaneous	Simultaneous effect flag	Boolean

Object Representation   None

Quality Criteria   None

Attribute Dependent Tests

Where Attribute: Structure = "EFFECT"

Mandatory Relationships	✓	Does the software tool ensure that each ECD Node
EEM54ADMR1		represents one and only one **Effect**? (3)
EEM54ADMR2		is the child of one and only one **ECD Node**? (3)

148

Chapter 8
Entity Event Modelling

Where Attribute: Structure = "SELECTION"

Mandatory Relationships	✓	Does the software tool ensure that each **ECD Node**
EEM54ADMR3		is the parent of *two* or more **ECD Node**? (3)

Where Attribute: Structure = "ITERATION"

Mandatory Relationships	✓	Does the software tool ensure that each **ECD Node**
EEM54ADMR4		is the parent of one and only one **ECD Node**? (3)

Where Attribute: Structure = "COMPOSITE"

Mandatory Relationships	✓	Does the software tool ensure that each **ECD Node**
EEM54ADMR5		is the parent of one or more **ECD Node**? (3)

Where Attribute: Structure = "ELEMENTARY"

Mandatory Relationships	✓	Does the software tool ensure that each **ECD Node**
EEM54ADMR6		is the child of one and only one **ECD Node**? (3)

Where Attribute: Structure = "SELECTION"

Optional Relationships	✓	Does the software tool allow an **ECD Node**
EEM54ADOR1		to be the child of one and only one **ECD Node**? (3)

Testing Criteria for the SSADM Version 4 Tools Conformance Scheme

Where Attribute: Structure = "ITERATION"

Optional Relationships	✓	Does the software tool allow an **ECD Node**
EEM54ADOR2		to be the child of one and only one **ECD Node**? (3)

Where Attribute: Structure = "COMPOSITE"

Optional Relationships	✓	Does the software tool allow an **ECD Node**
EEM54ADOR3		to be the child of one and only one **ECD Node**? (3)

Where Attribute: Structure = "EFFECT"

Object Representation	✓	Does the software tool ensure that each **ECD Node** has the following object representation for the given attribute value?
EEM54ADOB1		Entity Name

Where Attribute: Structure = "SELECTION"

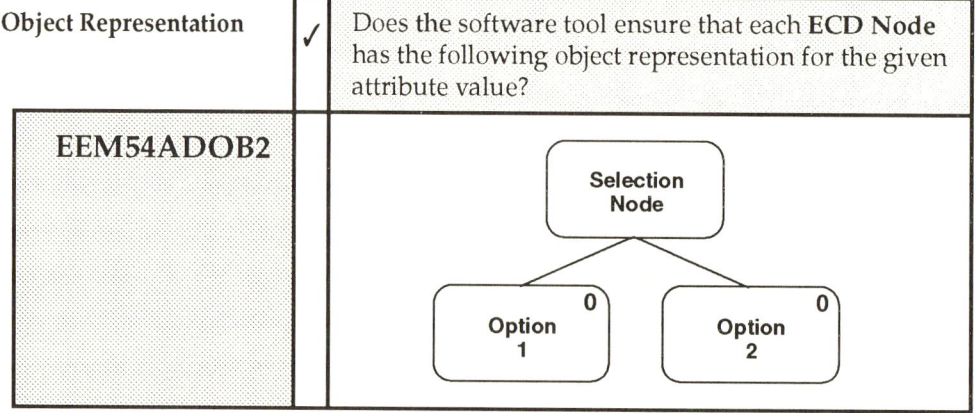

150

Chapter 8
Entity Event Modelling

Where Attribute: Structure = "ITERATION"

Object Representation	✓	Does the software tool ensure that each **ECD Node** has the following object representation for the given attribute value?
EEM54ADOB3		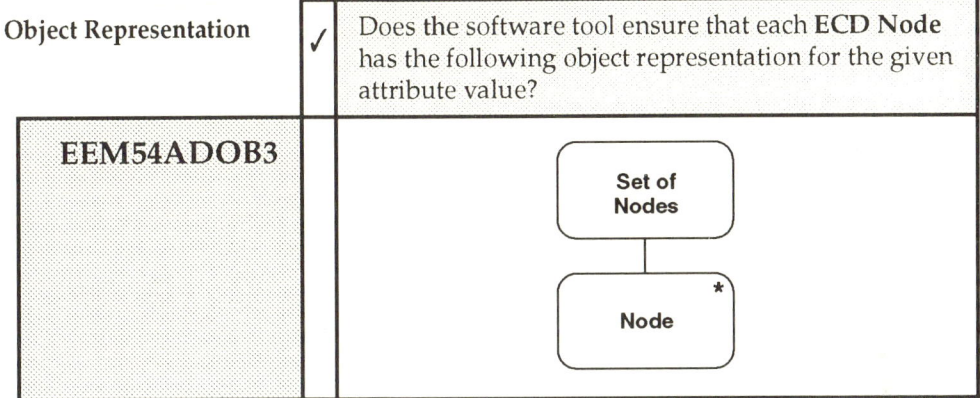

Where Attribute: Simultaneous = "TRUE"

Object Representation	✓	Does the software tool ensure that each **ECD Node** has the following object representation for the given attribute value?
EEM54ADOB4		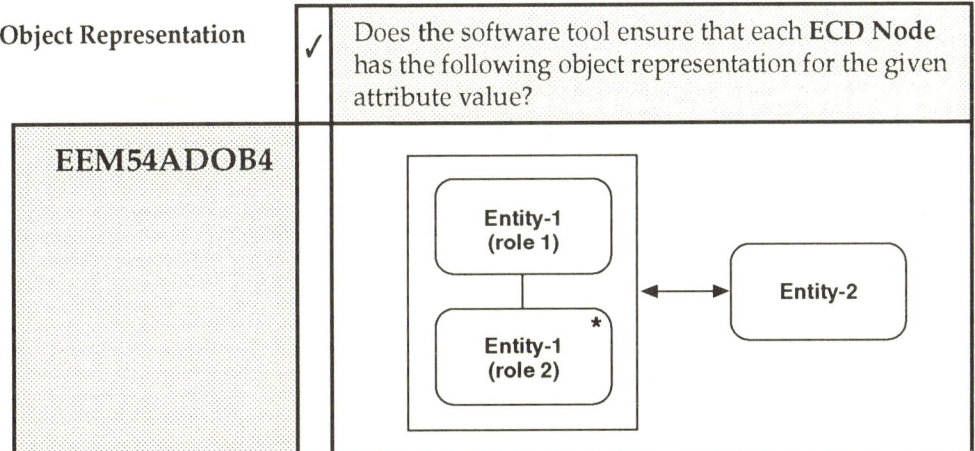

Where Attribute: Structure = "EFFECT"

Quality Criteria	✓	Which of the following quality criteria does the software tool enforce?
EEM54ADQC1		Attribute: Type = "ELEMENTARY" (3)
EEM54ADQC2		The ECD NODE must have no children (3)

Where Attribute: Structure = "SELECTION"

Quality Criteria	✓	Which of the following quality criteria does the software tool enforce?
EEM54ADQC3		Attribute: Type = "COMPOSITE" (3)

Where Attribute: Structure = "ITERATION"

Quality Criteria	✓	Which of the following quality criteria does the software tool enforce?
EEM54ADQC4		Attribute: Type = "COMPOSITE" (3)

EEM55 Effect Qualifier

Each **Effect Qualifier** has significance as qualifying an effect where the one event can affect one entity occurrence in more than one way. (3)

Mandatory Relationships	✓	Does the software tool ensure that each **Effect Qualifier**
EEM55MR1		is for one and only one **Effect**? (3)

Optional Relationships   None

Attributes		✓	Which of the following attributes for each **Effect Qualifier** does the software tool support?	
			Name	Description	Validation
	EEM55A1		Condition	Effect condition	Text

Chapter 8
Entity Event Modelling

Object Representation	✓	Does the software tool ensure that each **Effect Qualifier** has the following object representation?
EEM55OB1		Entity Life History Notation — Event Name (Qualifier) Effect Correspondence Diagram Notation — Entity Name (Qualifier)

Quality Criteria None

Attribute Dependent Tests

Mandatory Relationships None

Optional Relationships None

Object Representation None

Quality Criteria None

EEM56 Effect Correspondence

Each **Effect Correspondence** has significance as showing the one-to-one association between ECD Nodes.(3)

Mandatory Relationships	✓	Does the software tool ensure that each **Effect Correspondence**
EEM56MR1		is drawn on one and only one **Effect Correspondence Diagram**? (3)
EEM56MR2		is sourced by one and only one **ECD Node**? (3)
EEM56MR3		is received by one and only one **ECD Node**? (3)

Optional Relationships		None		
Attributes	✓	Which of the following attributes for each **Effect Correspondence** does the software tool support?		
		Name	Description	Validation
EEM56A1		Identifier	Source and destination nodes	Names of two existing ECD nodes

Object Representation	✓	Does the software tool ensure that each **Effect Correspondence** has the following object representation?
EEM56OB1		⟷

Quality Criteria   None

Attribute Dependent Tests

Mandatory Relationships   None

Optional Relationships   None

Object Representation   None

Quality Criteria   None

Chapter 8
Entity Event Modelling

EEM57 Entity Role

Each **Entity Role** has significance as stating the role of an effect when one event affects more than one entity occurrence of the same entity type. (3)

Mandatory Relationships	✓	Does the software tool ensure that each **Entity Role**
EEM57MR1		shows the further qualification of one and only one **Effect**? (3)

Optional Relationships   None

Attributes		✓	Which of the following attributes for each **Entity Role** does the software tool support?	
			Name	Description	Validation
EEM57A1			Role	Role of effect	Text

Object Representation	✓	Does the software tool ensure that each **Entity Role** has the following object representation?
EEM57OB1		Entity Life History Notation — Event Name (Role) Effect Correspondence Diagram Notation — Entity Name (Role)

Quality Criteria   None

Attribute Dependent Tests

Mandatory Relationships   None

Testing Criteria for the SSADM
Version 4 Tools Conformance Scheme

Optional Relationships   None

Object Representation   None

Quality Criteria   None

EEM58 ELH Operation

Each **ELH Operation** has significance as a discrete component of processing. An operation is a component of an effect. (3)

Mandatory Relationships	✓	Does the software tool ensure that each **ELH Operation**
EEM58MR1		is a component of one or more **Effect**? (3)
EEM58MR2		is represented by one or more **ELH Node**? (3)

Optional Relationships   None

Chapter 8
Entity Event Modelling

Attributes	✓	Which of the following attributes for each **ELH Operation** does the software tool support?		
		Name	Description	Validation
EEM58A1		Identifier	Entity Name + Operation Number	Name of existing entity + a Cardinal
EEM58A2		Description	Description of operation	Text
EEM58A3		Type	Type of operation	Store <Attribute>/ Store <Keys>/ Store Remaining <Attribute>/ Store <Attribute> Using <Expression>/ Replace <Attribute>/ Replace <Attribute> Using <Expression>/ Tie to <Entity>/ Cut from <Entity>/ Gain <Entity>/ Lose <Entity>

Object Representation	✓	Does the software tool ensure that each **ELH Operation** has the following object representation?
EEM58OB1		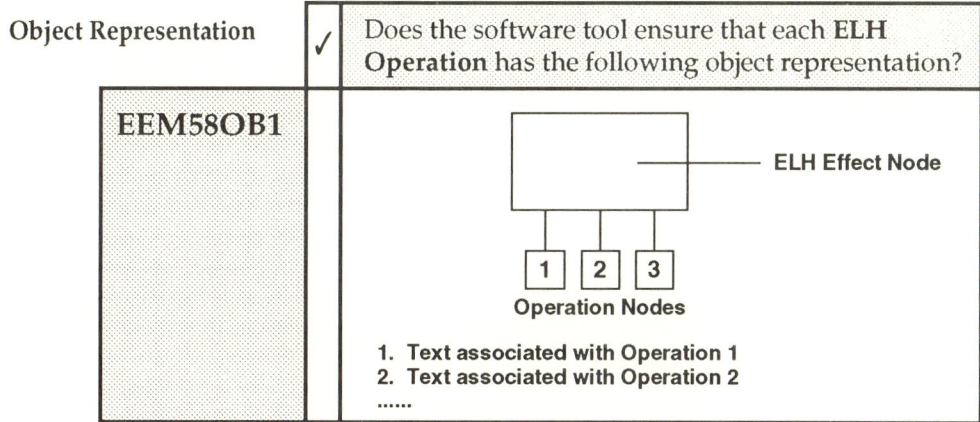

157

Quality Criteria	✓	Which of the following quality criteria does the software tool enforce?
EEM58QC1		The value of <Attribute> must be an attribute belonging to the Entity in the identifier

Attribute Dependent Tests

Mandatory Relationships   None

Optional Relationships   None

Object Representation   None

Quality Criteria   None

EEM59 Pre/Post State Indicator Value

Each **Pre/Post State Indicator Value** has significance as the values of a state indicator for an entity before and after the occurrence of an event. These may be displayed on ELH Elementary nodes. (5)

Mandatory Relationships	✓	Does the software tool ensure that each **Pre/Post State Indicator Value**
EEM59MR1		is assigned to one or more **Effect**? (5)
EEM59MR2		is documented by one and only one **ELH Node**? (5)

Optional Relationships   None

Chapter 8
Entity Event Modelling

Attributes	✓	Which of the following attributes for each **Pre/Post State Indicator Value** does the software tool support?		
		Name	Description	Validation
EEM59A1		Previous SIV	List of the valid previous SIVs	Cardinal or '-'
EEM59A2		Post SIV	Value after the completion of the operations	Cardinal or '-'
EEM59A3		Status	Primary or Secondary SIVs	PRIMARY / SECONDARY‡

Object Representation   None

Quality Criteria   None

Attribute Dependent Tests

Mandatory Relationships   None

Optional Relationships   None

Where Attribute: Status = "PRIMARY"

Object Representation	✓	Does the software tool ensure that each **Pre/Post State Indicator Value** has the following object representation for the given attribute value?
EEM59ADOB1		⬜———— ELH Effect Node Primary SIV Pre SIVs/Post SIV

159

Testing Criteria for the SSADM
Version 4 Tools Conformance Scheme

Where Attribute: Status = "SECONDARY"

Object Representation	✓	Does the software tool ensure that each **Pre/Post State Indicator Value** has the following object representation for the given attribute value?
EEM59ADOB2		▢ ── ELH Effect Node Primary SIV Pre SIVs/Post SIV Secondary SIV (Pre SIVs/Post SIV)

Quality Criteria   None

EEM60 ELH Structure

Each **ELH Structure** has significance as a hierarchical structure for an entity life history. (3)

Mandatory Relationships	✓	Does the software tool ensure that each **ELH Structure**
EEM60MR1		is part of one and only one **Entity Life History**? (3)
EEM60MR2		contains one or more **ELH Node**? (3)

Optional Relationships   None

Attributes		✓	Which of the following attributes for each **ELH Structure** does the software tool support?	
			Name	Description	Validation
EEM60A1			Identifier	ID of structure	Unique
EEM60A2			Type	Type of Structure	ENTITY/ RANDOM EVENT

Object Representation   None

160

Chapter 8
Entity Event Modelling

Quality Criteria None

Attribute Dependent Tests

Where Attribute: Type = "RANDOM EVENT"

Mandatory Relationships	✓	Does the software tool ensure that each **ELH Structure**
EEM60ADMR1		defines the life history for one and only one **Event**? (3)
EEM60ADMR2		must be associated with one and only one **ELH Structure**? (3)

Where Attribute: Type = "ENTITY"

Optional Relationships	✓	Does the software tool allow an **ELH Structure**
EEM60ADOR1		to be associated with one or more **ELH Structure**? (3)

Where Attribute: Type = "ENTITY"

Object Representation	✓	Does the software tool ensure that each **ELH Structure** has the following object representation for the given attribute value?
EEM60ADOB1		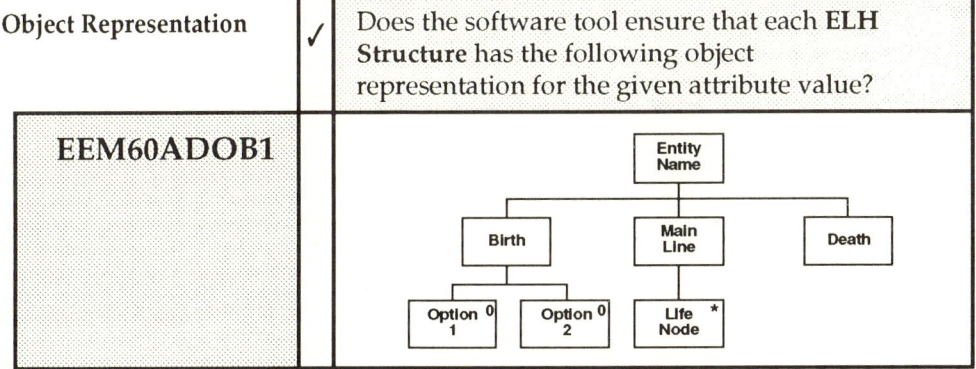

161

Where Attribute: Type = "RANDOM EVENT"

Object Representation	✓	Does the software tool ensure that each **ELH Structure** has the following object representation for the given attribute value?
EEM60ADOB2		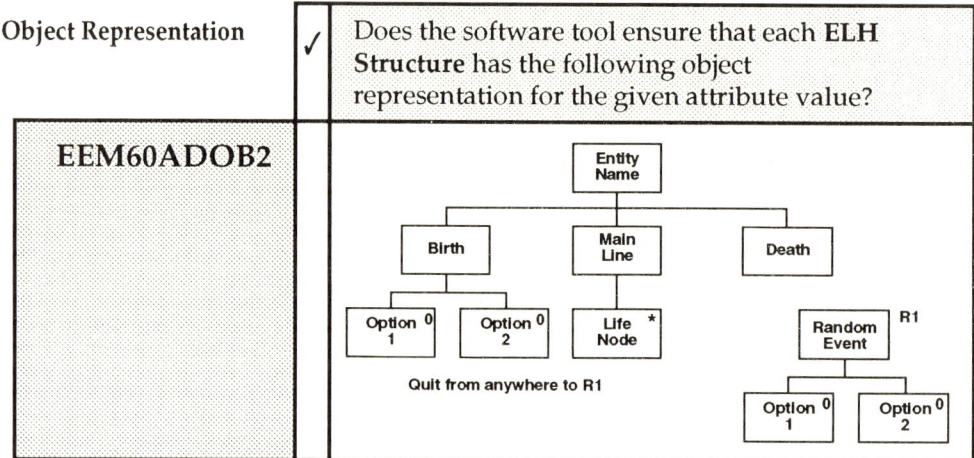

Where Attribute: Type = "RANDOM EVENT"

Quality Criteria	✓	Which of the following quality criteria does the software tool enforce?
EEM60ADQC1		The ELH Structure must not contain a Quit Identifier which will resume on the ENTITY ELH Structure? (3)

Chapter 8
Entity Event Modelling

EEM61 Event/Entity Matrix Entry

Each **Event/Entity Matrix Entry** has significance as the effect of a single event on a single entity type. (3)

Mandatory Relationships	✓	Does the software tool ensure that each **Event/Entity Matrix**
EEM61MR1		belongs to one and only one **Event/Entity Matrix Entry**? (3)
EEM61MR2		references one and only one **Event**? (3)
EEM61MR3		references one and only one **Entity Type**? (3)

Optional Relationships   None

Attributes	✓	Which of the following attributes for each **Event/Entity Matrix** does the software tool support?		
		Name	Description	Validation
EEM61A1		Event	Event ID	ID of existing event
EEM61A2		Entity	Entity ID	ID of existing entity
EEM61A3		Cell Value	Corresponding entry value	'C', 'M', 'D', null or a combination

Object Representation   None

Quality Criteria   None

Attribute Dependent Tests

Mandatory Relationships   None

163

Testing Criteria for the SSADM
Version 4 Tools Conformance Scheme

Optional Relationships   None

Object Representation   None

Quality Criteria   None

9 Function Definition

This chapter contains tests for the following products and concepts:

Products

FDF1	Enquiry Access Path	166
FDF2	Function Definition	168
FDF3	Function Definitions (set)	171
FDF4	not used	
FDF5	I/O Structure	173
FDF6	I/O Structure Description	174
FDF7	I/O Structure Diagram	176
FDF8	I/O Structures (for all functions)	177

Concepts

FDF51	Function	178
FDF52	EAP Node	180
FDF53	Enquiry Trigger	185
FDF54	Access Path	186
FDF55	I/O Structure Diagram Node	187
FDF56	I/O Structure Element	193

FDF1 Enquiry Access Path

Each **Enquiry Access Path** has significance as the route through the Logical Data Model from an entry point to the entity, or entities, required for a particular enquiry function. (3)

Mandatory Relationships	✓	Does the software tool ensure that each **Enquiry Access Path**
FDF1MR1		shows the accesses for one or more **Function**? (3)
FDF1MR2		belongs to one and only one **Function Definition**? (3)
FDF1MR3		contains one or more **EAP Node**? (3)
FDF1MR4		contains one and only one **Enquiry Trigger**? (3)
FDF1MR5		is the basis for one and only one **Enquiry Process Model**? (3)

Optional Relationships	✓	Does the software tool allow an **Enquiry Access Path**
FDF1OR1		to contain one or more **Access Path**? (3)

Attributes		✓	Which of the following attributes for each **Enquiry Access Path** does the software tool support?	
			Name	Description	Validation
FDF1A1			Identifier	ID of function being described	ID of existing function

Chapter 9
Function Definition

Object Representation	✓	Does the software tool ensure that each **Enquiry Access Path** has the following object representation?
FDF1OB1		An **Enquiry Access Path** consists of • EAP Node • Enquiry Trigger • Access Path

Quality Criteria	✓	Which of the following quality criteria does the software tool enforce?
FDF1QC1		Is the data structure visible on the Logical Data Structure? (3)

Attribute Dependent Tests

Mandatory Relationships   None

Optional Relationships   None

Object Representation   None

Quality Criteria   None

167

FDF2   Function Definition

Each **Function Definition** has significance as defining a function which is to be provided by the required system. To draw together the SSADM documentation which describes the components of a function. To provide a user view of the system processing in preparation for further process design. (3,6) (5)

Mandatory Relationships	✓	Does the software tool ensure that each **Function Definition**
FDF2MR1		defines one and only one **Function**? (3,6)
FDF2MR2		references one and only one **Functional Requirement**? (3)
FDF2MR3		is documented by one or more **I/O Structure**? (3)

Optional Relationships	✓	Does the software tool allow a **Function Definition**
FDF2OR1		to reference one or more **Function**? (3,6)
FDF2OR2		to be further described by one or more **Service Level Requirement**? (3)
FDF2OR3		to be the reference for one or more **Common Process**? (3)
FDF2OR4		to reference one or more **Dialogue**? (5)
FDF2OR5		to reference one or more **User Role**? (3)

Chapter 9
Function Definition

Attributes	✓	Which of the following attributes for each **Function Definition** does the software tool support?		
		Name	Description	Validation
FDF2A1		Identifier	ID of function	Unique
FDF2A2		Function Name	Name of function	Text‡
FDF2A3		Process Type	Update/Enquiry	'U'/'E'‡
FDF2A4		Implementation Type	On-line/Off-line	'ON'/'OFF'‡
FDF2A5		Initiation Type	User/System	'U'/'S'‡
FDF2A6		Description	Description of function	'Text
FDF2A7		Error Description	Error handling descriptions	'Text
FDF2A8		DFD Processes	List of process references	Existing Process IDs
FDF2A9		Event (Repeating Group)		
		Event ID	ID of event	Existing event
		Frequency	Frequency of event	Text
FDF2A10		I/O Descriptions	List of I/O Description references	Existing I/O Descriptions
FDF2A11		Volumes	Frequency information	Text
FDF2A12		Related Functions	Reference to functions	Existing functions
FDF2A13		Enquiries (Repeating Group)		
		Enquiry	Enquiry Name	Existing enquiry
		Frequency	Frequency of Enquiry	Text

Testing Criteria for the SSADM
Version 4 Tools Conformance Scheme

Object Representation   none

Quality Criteria   None

Attribute Dependent Tests

Where Attribute: Process Type = 'U'

Mandatory Relationships	✓	Does the software tool ensure that each **Function Definition**
FDF2ADMR1		references one or more **DFD Process**? (3)
FDF2ADMR2		references one or more **I/O Description**? (3)
FDF2ADMR3		references one or more **Event**? (3)

Where Attribute: Implementation Type = 'ON'

Mandatory Relationships	✓	Does the software tool ensure that each **Function Definition**
FDF2ADMR4		references one or more **User Role**? (3)
FDF2ADMR5		references one or more **Dialogue**? (5)

Where Attribute: Process Type = 'E'

Optional Relationships	✓	Does the software tool allow a **Function Definition**
FDF2ADOR1		to reference one or more **DFD Process**? (3)
FDF2ADOR2		to be the reference for enquiry of one or more **Function**? (3)

Object Representation   None

Chapter 9
Function Definition

Where Attribute: Process Type = 'E'

Quality Criteria	✓	Which of the following quality criteria does the software tool enforce?
FDF2ADQC1		Is the function specified without a list of events? (3)

Where Attribute: Process Type = 'U'

Quality Criteria	✓	Which of the following quality criteria does the software tool enforce?
FDF2ADQC2		Does the function include one or more events? (3)

FDF3 Function Definitions

Each **Function Definitions** has significance as packaging all of the details about functions to be included the Requirements Specification. (3,6) (5)

Mandatory Relationships	✓	Does the software tool ensure that each **Function Definitions**
FDF3MR1		belongs to one and only one **Physical Process Specification**? (6)
FDF3MR2		belongs to one and only one **Processing Specification**? (3)
FDF3MR3		belongs to one and only one **Logical Process Model**? (5)
FDF3MR4		contains one and only one **I/O Structures** (for all functions)? (3)

171

Testing Criteria for the SSADM
Version 4 Tools Conformance Scheme

Optional Relationships	✓	Does the software tool allow each **Function Definitions**		
FDF3OR1		to contain one or more **Elementary Process Description**? (3)		

Attributes	✓	Which of the following attributes for each **Function Definitions** does the software tool support?		
		Name	Description	Validation
FDF3A1		Name	Name of Set	Unique

Object Representation	✓	Does the software tool ensure that each **Function Definitions** has the following object representation?
FDF3OB1		A **Function Definitions** consists of A set of **Function Definition** A set of **Elementary Process Description**

Quality Criteria	✓	Which of the following quality criteria does the software tool enforce?
FDF3QC1		Are the cross-references to/from common processing descriptions and function definitions complete and correct? (3)
FDF3QC2		Are all referenced common Elementary Process Descriptions included in the set? (3)

Attribute Dependent Tests

Mandatory Relationships None

Optional Relationships None

Object Representation None

Quality Criteria None

FDF5 I/O Structure

Each **I/O Structure** has significance as documenting the input to and outputs from a function, or part of a function. (3)

Mandatory Relationships	✓	Does the software tool ensure that each **I/O Structure**
FDF5MR1		belongs to one and only one **I/O Structures** (for all functions)? (3)
FDF5MR2		contains one and only one **I/O Structure Diagram**? (3)
FDF5MR3		contains one and only one **I/O Structure Description**? (3)
FDF5MR4		documents one and only one **Function Definition**? (3)

Optional Relationships   None

Attributes	✓	Which of the following attributes for each **I/O Structure** does the software tool support?		
		Name	Description	Validation
FDF5A1		Identifier	ID of I/O Structure	Function ID + cardinal
FDF5A2		Name	Name of I/O Structure	Unique

Object Representation	✓	Does the software tool ensure that each **I/O Structure** has the following object representation?

FDF5OB1		An **I/O Structure** consists of
		    An **I/O Structure Diagram**
		    An **I/O Structure Description**

Testing Criteria for the SSADM
Version 4 Tools Conformance Scheme

Quality Criteria	✓	Which of the following quality criteria does the software tool enforce?
FDF5QC1		Are all I/O Structure elements on the I/O Structure Diagram documented on the I/O Structure Description? (3)
FDF5QC2		Does the I/O Structure Description describe only elements on the I/O Structure Diagram? (3)

Attribute Dependent Tests

Mandatory Relationships   None

Optional Relationships   None

Object Representation   None

Quality Criteria   None

FDF6   I/O Structure Description

Each **I/O Structure Description** has significance as documenting the I/O Structure down to data item level. (3)

Mandatory Relationships	✓	Does the software tool ensure that each **I/O Structure Description**
FDF6MR1		belongs to one and only one **I/O Structure**? (3)
FDF6MR2		references one or more **Data Flow**? (3)
FDF6MR3		contains one or more **I/O Structure Element**? (3)

Optional Relationships   None

Chapter 9
Function Definition

Attributes	✓	Which of the following attributes for each I/O Structure Description does the software tool support?		
		Name	Description	Validation
FDF6A1		Identifier	ID of I/O Structure	Existing I/O Structure
FDF6A2		Data flows	List of data flow referenced	Existing data flow IDs

Object Representation   None

Quality Criteria   None

Attribute Dependent Tests

Mandatory Relationships   None

Optional Relationships   None

Object Representation   None

Quality Criteria   None

175

FDF7 I/O Structure Diagram

Each **I/O Structure Diagram** has significance as showing graphically the sequencing of data items or groups of data items within the data flows into and out of functions. (3)

Mandatory Relationships	✓	Does the software tool ensure that each **I/O Structure Diagram**
FDF7MR1		belongs to one and only one **I/O Structure**? (3)
FDF7MR2		describes one or more **Data Flow**? (3)
FDF7MR3		contains one or more **I/O Structure Diagram Node**? (3)

Optional Relationships None

Attributes	✓	Which of the following attributes for each **I/O Structure Diagram** does the software tool support?		
		Name	Description	Validation
FDF7A1		Identifier	ID of Diagram	Function ID + Cardinal

Object Representation	✓	Does the software tool ensure that each **I/O Structure Diagram** has the following object representation?
FDF7OB1		An **I/O Structure Diagram** consists of: **I/O Structure Diagram Node**

Quality Criteria None

Attribute Dependent Tests

Mandatory Relationships None

Optional Relationships None

Chapter 9
Function Definition

Object Representation   None

Quality Criteria   None

FDF8   I/O Structures (for all functions)

Each **I/O Structures (for all functions)** has significance as packaging all I/O Structures for all identified functions. (3)

Mandatory Relationships	✓	Does the software tool ensure that each **I/O Structures (for all functions)**	
FDF8MR1		contains one or more **I/O Structure**? (3)	
FDF8MR2		belongs to one and only one **Function Definitions**? (3)	

Optional Relationships   None

Attributes	✓	Which of the following attributes for each **I/O Structures (for all functions)** does the software tool support?		
		Name	Description	Validation
FDF8A1		Identifier	Group Name	Text

Object Representation   None

Quality Criteria   None

Attribute Dependent Tests

Mandatory Relationships   None

Optional Relationships   None

177

Testing Criteria for the SSADM
Version 4 Tools Conformance Scheme

Object Representation None

Quality Criteria None

FDF51 Function

Each **Function** has significance as a set of system processing which the users wish to schedule together to support their business activity. (3,6)

Mandatory Relationships	✓	Does the software tool ensure that each **Function**
FDF51MR1		is defined by one and only one **Function Definition**? (3,6)

Optional Relationships	✓	Does the software tool allow a **Function**
FDF51OR1		to be referenced by one or more **Function Definition**? (3,6)

Attributes		✓	Which of the following attributes for each **Function** does the software tool support?	
		Name	Description	Validation
FDF51A1		Identifier	ID of function	Unique
FDF51A2		Name	Name of function	Text
FDF51A3		Process Type	Update/Enquiry	'U'/'E'
FDF51A4		Implementation	On-line/Off-line	ON /OFF Type
FDF51A5		Initiation Type	User/System	'U'/'S'

Object Representation None

Chapter 9
Function Definition

Quality Criteria	✓	Which of the following quality criteria does the software tool enforce?
FDF51QC1		Is the function identifier unique? (3,6)
FDF51QC2		Is the function classified according to all three types: • update or enquiry • on-line or off-line • user or system initiated? (3,6)

Attribute Dependent Tests

Where attribute: Process Type = 'E'

Mandatory Relationships	✓	Does the software tool ensure that each **Function**
FDF51ADMR1		has its accesses shown by one and only one **Enquiry Access Path**? (3)

Where attribute: Implementation Type = 'ON' and Initiation Type = 'u'

Mandatory Relationships	✓	Does the software tool ensure that each **Function**
FDF51ADMR2		is referenced by one or more **User Role/Function Matrix Entry**? (3)

Where attribute: Process Type = 'u'

Optional Relationships	✓	Does the software tool allow a **Function**
FDF51ADOR1		to have its accesses shown by one or more **Enquiry Access Path**? (3)

Where attribute: Implementation Type = 'ON' and Initiation Type = 'u'

Optional Relationships	✓	Does the software tool allow a **Function**
FDF51ADOR2		to be the subject of one or more **Prototype Pathway**? (3)

Object Representation   None

Quality Criteria   None

FDF52 EAP Node

Each **EAP Node** has significance as a node on an Enquiry Access Path. Each node is one of the following types:

- a composite node
- an elementary node.

Each node must have one of the following structures:

- an entity node
- a selection node
- an iteration node. (3)

Mandatory Relationships	✓	Does the software tool ensure that each **EAP Node**
FDF52MR1		belongs to one and only one **Enquiry Access Path**? (3)

Optional Relationships	✓	Does the software tool allow an **EAP Node**
FDF52OR1		to relate to the occurrences of one and only one **Entity Type**? (3)
FDF52OR2		to be sourced by one or more **Access Path**? (3)
FDF52OR3		to be targeted to one or more **Access Path**? (3)

Chapter 9
Function Definition

Attributes	✓	Which of the following attributes for each **EAP Node** does the software tool support?		
		Name	**Description**	**Validation**
FDF52A1		Name	Name of node	Text
FDF52A2		Type	Type of node	COMPOSITE/ ELEMENTARY
FDF52A3		Structure	Structure of node	SEQUENCE/ SELECTION/ ITERATION

Object Representation   None

Quality Criteria   None

Attribute Dependent Tests

Where attribute: Type = "COMPOSITE"

Mandatory Relationships	✓	Does the software tool ensure that each **EAP Node**
FDF52ADMR1		is the parent of one or more **EAP Node**? (3)

Where attribute: Type = "ELEMENTARY"

Mandatory Relationships	✓	Does the software tool ensure that each **EAP Node**
FDF52ADMR2		is the child of one and only one **EAP Node**? (3)

Where attribute: Type = "SELECTION"

Mandatory Relationships	✓	Does the software tool ensure that each **EAP Node**
FDF52ADMR3		is the parent of *two* or more **EAP Node**? (3)

Where attribute: Type = "ITERATION"

Mandatory Relationships	✓	Does the software tool ensure that each **EAP Node**
FDF52ADMR4		is the parent of one and only one **EAP Node**? (3)

Where attribute: Type = "COMPOSITE"

Optional Relationships	✓	Does the software tool allow an **EAP Node**
FDF52ADOR1		to be the child of one and only one **EAP Node**? (3)

Where attribute: Type = "SEQUENCE"

Optional Relationships	✓	Does the software tool allow an **EAP Node**
FDF52ADOR2		to be the parent of one or more **EAP Node**? (3)
FDF52ADOR3		to be the child of one and only one **EAP Node**? (3)

Where attribute: Type = "SELECTION"

Optional Relationships	✓	Does the software tool allow an **EAP Node**
FDF52ADOR4		to be the child of one and only one **EAP Node**? (3)

Chapter 9
Function Definition

Where attribute: Type = "ITERATION"

Optional Relationships	✓	Does the software tool allow an **EAP Node**
FDF52ADOR5		to be the child of one and only one **EAP Node**? (3)

Where Attribute: Structure = "SEQUENCE"

Object Representation	✓	Does the software tool ensure that each **EAP Node** has the following object representation for the given attribute value?
FDF52ADOB1		(Entity Name)

Where Attribute: Structure = "SELECTION"

Object Representation	✓	Does the software tool ensure that each **EAP Node** has the following object representation for the given attribute value?
FDF52ADOB2		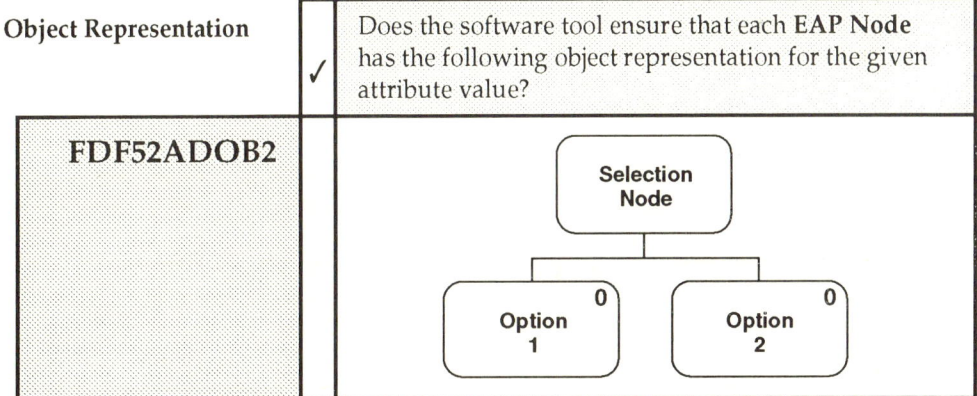

183

Where Attribute: Structure = "ELEMENTARY"

Object Representation	✓	Does the software tool ensure that each **EAP Node** has the following object representation for the given attribute value?
FDF52ADOB3		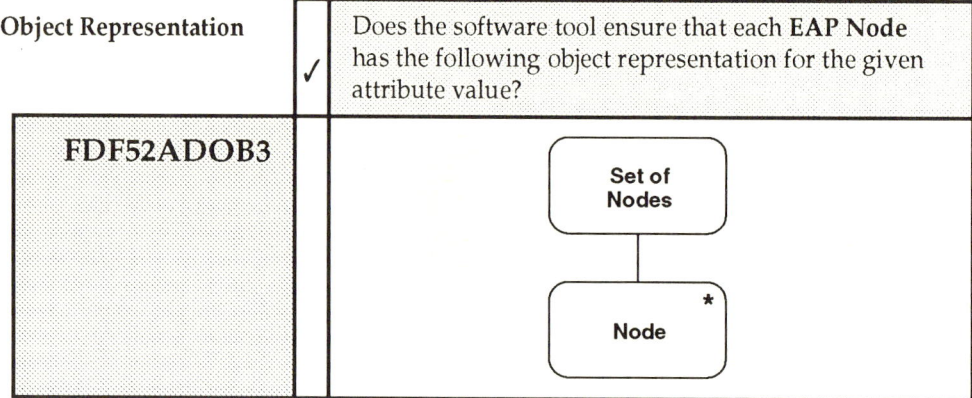

Where Attribute: Structure = "SELECTION"

Quality Criteria	✓	Which of the following quality criteria does the software tool enforce?
FDF52ADQC1		Attribute: Type = "COMPOSITE" (3)

Where Attribute: Structure = "ITERATION"

Quality Criteria	✓	Which of the following quality criteria does the software tool enforce?
FDF52ADQC2		Attribute: Type = "COMPOSITE" Attribute: Name = "Set of <Entity>"(3)

Where Attribute: Structure = "ELEMENTARY"

Quality Criteria	✓	Which of the following quality criteria does the software tool enforce?
FDF52ADQC3		The **EAP Node** must have no children (3)

Chapter 9
Function Definition

FDF53 Enquiry Trigger

Each **Enquiry Trigger** has significance as a set of data items for which values are input to a system to initiate an instance of an enquiry function. (3)

Mandatory Relationships	✓	Does the software tool ensure that each **Enquiry Trigger**
FDF53MR1		triggers one and only one **Enquiry Access Path**? (3)

Optional Relationships	✓	Does the software tool allow an **Enquiry Trigger**
FDF53OR1		to contain one or more **Attribute Type**? (3)

Attributes		✓	Which of the following attributes for each **Enquiry Trigger** does the software tool support?	
		Name	Description	Validation
FDF53A1		Entry key	The key or index used for initial access	Existing attribute types

Object Representation	✓	Does the software tool ensure that each **Enquiry Trigger** has the following object representation?
FDF53OB1		Key Attribute → Entity Name

Quality Criteria None

Attribute Dependent Tests

Mandatory Relationships None

Testing Criteria for the SSADM
Version 4 Tools Conformance Scheme

Optional Relationships   None

Object Representation   None

Quality Criteria   None

FDF54 Access Path

Each **Access Path** has significance as showing an access on an Enquiry Access Path. (3)

Mandatory Relationships	✓	Does the software tool ensure that each **Access Path**
FDF54MR1		belongs to one and only one **Enquiry Access Path**? (3)
FDF54MR2		is the source of an access of one and only one **EAP Node**? (3)
FDF54MR3		is the target of an access of one and only one **EAP Node**? (3)

Optional Relationships   None

Attributes	✓	Which of the following attributes for each **Access Path** does the software tool support?		
		Name	Description	Validation
FDF54A1		Identifier	Identifier of access path	Names of source and destination node

Object Representation	✓	Does the software tool ensure that each **Access Path** has the following object representation?
FDF54OB1		⟶

Quality Criteria   None

Attribute Dependent Tests

Mandatory Relationships None

Optional Relationships None

Object Representation None

Quality Criteria None

FDF55 I/O Structure Diagram Node

Each **I/O Structure Diagram Node** has significance as a node on an I/O Structure Diagram. Each node is one of the following types:

- a root node
- an intermediate node
- an elementary node (3)

Each node must have one of the following structures:

- a sequence node
- a selection node
- an iteration node
- a leaf node (3)

Mandatory Relationships	✓	Does the software tool ensure that each **I/O Structure Diagram Node**
FDF55MR1		is part of one and only one **I/O Structure Diagram**? (3)

Optional Relationships	✓	Does the software tool allow each **I/O Structure Diagram Node**
FDF55OR1		to be the child of one and only one **I/O Structure Diagram Node**? (3)
FDF55OR2		to be the parent of one or more **I/O Structure Diagram Node**? (3)

Testing Criteria for the SSADM
Version 4 Tools Conformance Scheme

Attributes	✓	Which of the following attributes for each **I/O Structure Diagram Node** does the software tool support?		
		Name	Description	Validation
FDF55A1		Name	Name of node	Text
FDF55A2		Type	Type of node	ROOT/ INTERMEDIATE /ELEMENTARY
FDF55A3		Structure	Structure of node	SEQUENCE/ SELECTION/ ITERATION/ LEAF

Object Representation   None

Quality Criteria   None

Attribute Dependent Tests

Where Attribute: Type = "ROOT"

Mandatory Relationships	✓	Does the software tool ensure that each **I/O Structure Diagram Node**
FDF55ADMR1		is in correspondence with one or more **Data Flow**? (3)
FDF55ADMR2		is the parent of one or more **I/O Structure Diagram Node**? (3)

Where Attribute: Type = "INTERMEDIATE"

Mandatory Relationships	✓	Does the software tool ensure that each I/O Structure Diagram Node
FDF55ADMR3		is the child of one and only one **I/O Structure Diagram Node**? (3)
FDF55ADMR4		is the parent of one or more **I/O Structure Diagram Node**? (3)

Where Attribute: Type = "ELEMENTARY"

Mandatory Relationships	✓	Does the software tool ensure that each I/O Structure Diagram Node
FDF55ADMR5		is the child of one and only one **I/O Structure Diagram Node**? (3)

Where Attribute: Type = "SEQUENCE"

Mandatory Relationships	✓	Does the software tool ensure that each I/O Structure Diagram Node
FDF55ADMR6		is the parent of *two* or more **I/O Structure Diagram Node**? (3)

Where Attribute: Type = "SELECTION"

Mandatory Relationships	✓	Does the software tool ensure that each I/O Structure Diagram Node
FDF55ADMR7		is the parent of *two* or more **I/O Structure Diagram Node**? (3)

Where Attribute: Type = "ITERATION"

Mandatory Relationships	✓	Does the software tool ensure that each **I/O Structure Diagram Node**
FDF55ADMR8		is the parent of one and only one **I/O Structure Diagram Node**? (3)

Where Attribute: Type = "LEAF"

Mandatory Relationships	✓	Does the software tool ensure that each **I/O Structure Diagram Node**
FDF55ADMR9		represents one and only one **I/O Structure Element**? (3)

Where Attribute: Type = "ROOT"

Object Representation	✓	Does the software tool ensure that each **I/O Structure Diagram Node** has the following object representation for the given attribute value?
FDF55ADOB1		Root node name

Where Attribute: Type = "SEQUENCE"

Object Representation	✓	Does the software tool ensure that each **I/O Structure Diagram Node** has the following object representation for the given attribute value?
FDF55ADOB2		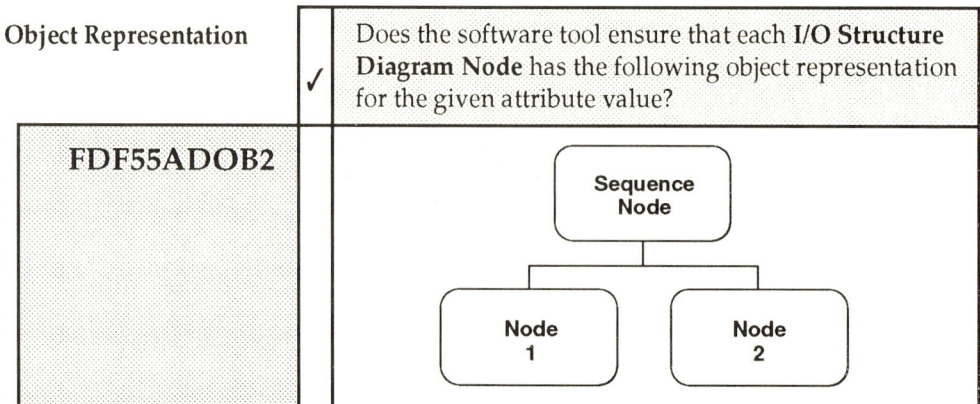

Chapter 9
Function Definition

Where Attribute: Type = "SELECTION"

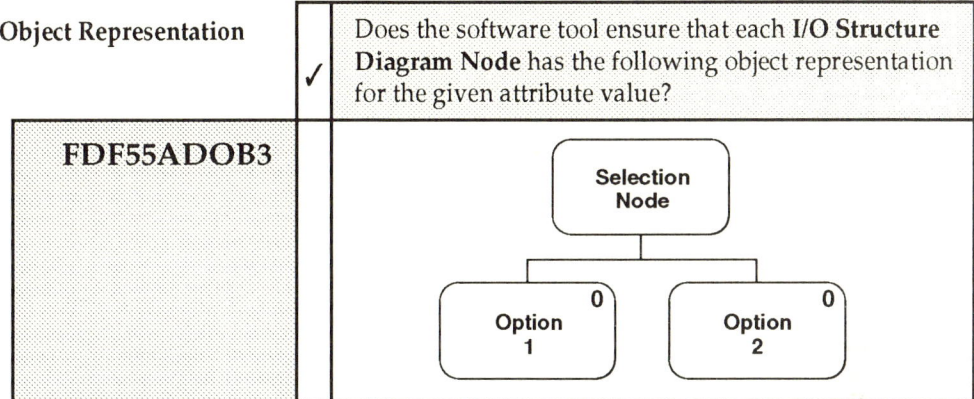

Where Attribute: Type = "ITERATION"

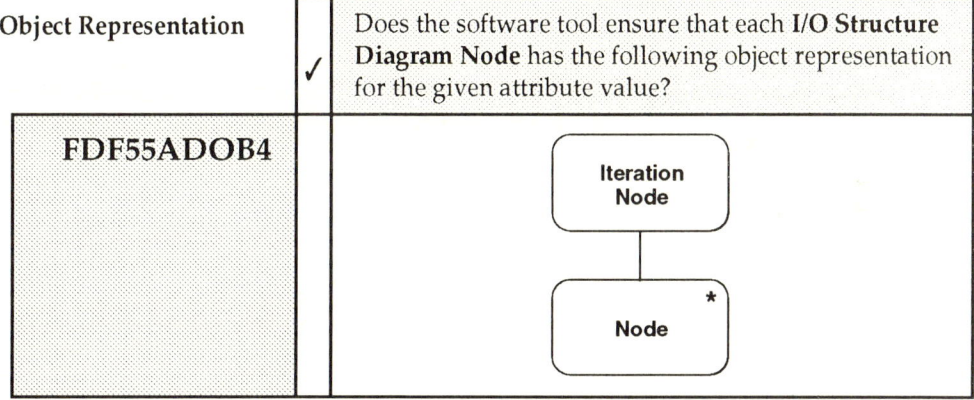

Where Attribute: Type = "LEAF"

Object Representation	✓	Does the software tool ensure that each **I/O Structure Diagram Node** has the following object representation for the given attribute value?
FDF55ADOB5		I/O Structure Element Name (Input/Output)

191

Testing Criteria for the SSADM
Version 4 Tools Conformance Scheme

Where Attribute: Type = "ELEMENTARY"

Quality Criteria	✓	Which of the following quality criteria does the software tool enforce?
FDF55ADQC1		Attribute: Structure = "LEAF" (3)

Where Attribute: Type = "SELECTION"

Quality Criteria	✓	Which of the following quality criteria does the software tool enforce?
FDF55ADQC2		Attribute: Type = "INTERMEDIATE" (3)

Where Attribute: Type = "ITERATION"

Quality Criteria	✓	Which of the following quality criteria does the software tool enforce?
FDF55ADQC3		Attribute: Type = "INTERMEDIATE" (3)

Where Attribute: Type = "LEAF"

Quality Criteria	✓	Which of the following quality criteria does the software tool enforce?
FDF55ADQC4		Attribute: Name = "<I/O Structure Element> + (input) or (output)" Attribute: Type = "ELEMENTARY" (3) The **I/O Structure Diagram Node** must have no children (3)

Chapter 9
Function Definition

FDF56 I/O Structure Element

Each **I/O Structure Element** has significance as describing the data items that form an I/O Structure. (3)

Mandatory Relationships	✓	Does the software tool ensure that each **I/O Structure Element**
FDF56MR1		is part of one and only one **I/O Structure Description**? (3)
FDF56MR2		is represented by one and only one **I/O Structure Diagram Node**? (3)
FDF56MR3		contains one or more **Attribute Type**? (3)

Optional Relationships   None

Attributes	✓	Which of the following attributes for each **I/O Structure Element** does the software tool support?		
		Name	Description	Validation
FDF56A1		Name	Name of element	Unique ID
FDF56A2		Data Items	List of attribute types	Existing attribute types
FDF56A3		Comment	Note	Text

Object Representation   None

Quality Criteria   None

Attribute Dependent Tests

Mandatory Relationships   None

Optional Relationships   None

Testing Criteria for the SSADM
Version 4 Tools Conformance Scheme

Object Representation None

Quality Criteria None

Chapter 10
Logical Data Modelling

10 Logical Data Modelling

This chapter contains tests for the following products and concepts:

Products

LDM1	Attribute/Data Item Description	196
LDM2	Data Catalogue	198
LDM3	Entity Description	200
LDM4	Grouped Domain Description	203
LDM5	Logical Data Model	205
LDM6	Logical Data Structure	209
LDM7	Relationship Description	210

Concepts

LDM51	Entity Type	213
LDM52	Relationship Type	215
LDM53	Relationship End	217
LDM54	Domain	220
LDM55	Attribute Type	222
LDM56	Exclusive Relationship Group	224

Testing Criteria for the SSADM
Version 4 Tools Conformance Scheme

LDM1 Attribute/Data Item Description

Each **Attribute/Data Item Description** has significance in that it describes all known details about an attribute (data item) in the logical system. Details are later translated into physical data item(s) for the implementation of the system. (0,1,3,5,6)

Mandatory Relationships	✓	Does the software tool ensure that each **Attribute/Data Item Description**
LDM1MR1		describes one and only one **Attribute Type**? (0,1,3,5,6)
LDM1MR2		belongs to one and only one **Data Catalogue**? (0,1,3,5,6)

Optional Relationships	✓	Does the software tool allow an **Attribute/Data Item Description**
LDM1OR1		to reference one or more **User Role**? (3)

Attributes		✓	Which of the following attributes for each **Attribute Data/Item Description** does the software tool support?		
			Name	Description	Validation
LDM1A1			Name	Name of attribute	Name of attribute - Unique
LDM1A2			Identifier	Reference name or number	ID of attribute type
LDM1A3			Cross-Reference (Repeating Group)		
			ID	ID of Cross-Reference	ID of existing SSADM document
			Type	Type of Cross-Reference	Text
LDM1A4			Synonyms	List of Synonyms	Text

196

Chapter 10
Logical Data Modelling

Attributes	✓	Which of the following attributes for each **Attribute Data/Item Description** does the software tool support?		
		Name	Description	Validation
LDM1A5		Description	Description of attribute	Text
LDM1A6		Validation/ Derivation	Validation and/ or derivation of the attribute	Text
LDM1A7		Status	Status of Attribute	MANDATORY /OPTIONAL
LDM1A8		Default value	Initialisation value	Only with MANDATORY status
LDM1A9		Null value	Value when not in use	Only with OPTIONAL status
LDM1A10		Logical format	Format of attribute	Numeric, char etc
LDM1A11		Unit of measure	Unit of length	Text
LDM1A12		Logical length	Length of Attribute	Text/Numeric
LDM1A13		Length Description	Describing variable lengths	Text
LDM1A14		Users - (Repeating Group)		
		User Role	User who have access	Existing User Role
		Access rights	Access rights of User	I,R,M,D,A,ALL
LDM1A15		Owner	Owner of Data	Person/User Role
LDM1A16		Standard Msg	Error/help message	Text
LDM1A17		Notes	Comment	Text

Object representation   None

Quality Criteria   None

197

Testing Criteria for the SSADM
Version 4 Tools Conformance Scheme

Attribute Dependent Tests

Mandatory Relationships   None

Optional Relationships   None

Object Representation   None

Quality Criteria   None

LDM2 Data Catalogue

Each **Data Catalogue** has significance as the central repository for all the descriptive information about items of data. This includes physical details which may be found during data flow modelling as well as physical design activities. (0,1,2,3,4,5,6)

Mandatory Relationships	✓	Does the software tool ensure that each **Data Catalogue**
LDM2MR1		belongs to one and only one **Current Services Description**? (1)
LDM2MR2		belongs to one and only one **Requirements Specification**? (3)
LDM2MR3		belongs to one and only one **Physical Process Specification**? (6)
LDM2MR4		Contains one or more **Attribute/Data Item Description**? (0,1,3,5,6)
LDM2MR5		belongs to one and only one **Logical Design**? (5)

Chapter 10
Logical Data Modelling

Optional Relationships	✓	Does the software tool allow a **Data Catalogue**		
LDM2OR1		to contain one or more **Grouped Domain Description**? (0,1,2,3,4,5,6)		

Attributes	✓	Which of the following attributes for each **Data Catalogue** does the software tool support?		
		Name	Description	Validation
LDM2A1		Name	ID of Catalogue	Unique

Object Representation	✓	Does the software tool ensure that each **Data Catalogue** has the following object representation?
LDM2OB1		A **Data Catalogue** is composed of A set of **Attribute/Data Item Description** A set of **Grouped Domain Descripton**

Quality Criteria	✓	Which of the following quality criteria does the software tool enforce?
LDM2QC1		Are any incomplete attribute types highlighted? (0,1,3,5,6)
LDM2QC2		Are any incomplete grouped domains highlighted? (0,1,2,3,4,5,6)

Attribute Dependent Tests

Mandatory Relationships None

Optional Relationships None

Object Representation None

Quality Criteria None

199

Testing Criteria for the SSADM
Version 4 Tools Conformance Scheme

LDM3 Entity Description

Each **Entity Description** has significance as documenting all of the details concerned with an entity on the Logical Data Structure, including details of state indicators which are applied during entity life history analysis. There will be associated Relationship Descriptions for each related entity on the Logical Data Structure. (0,1,3,5)

Mandatory Relationships	✓	Does the software tool ensure that each **Entity Description**
LDM3MR1		describes one and only one **Entity Type**? (0,1,3,5)
LDM3MR2		contains one or more **Attribute Type**? (0,1,3,5)
LDM3MR3		contains one or more **Relationship Type**? (0,1,3)
LDM3MR4		belongs to one and only one **Logical Data Model**? (0,1,3,5)

Optional Relationships	✓	Does the software tool allow an **Entity Description**
LDM3OR1		to reference one or more **User Role**? (3)

Attributes	✓	Which of the following attributes for each **Entity Description** does the software tool support?		
		Name	Description	Validation
LDM3A1		Variant	Name of Logical Data Model variant	'OUTLINE'/ 'CURRENT ENVIRONMENT' /'REQUIRED SYSTEM'
LDM3A2		Identifier	ID of entity	ID of existing entity
LDM3A3		Name	Name of entity	Name of existing entity

Chapter 10
Logical Data Modelling

Attributes	✓	Which of the following attributes for each **Entity Description** does the software tool support?		
		Name	**Description**	**Validation**
LDM3A4		Location	For distributed systems	Text
LDM3A5		Ave. Occurrence	Average Occurence	Numeric
LDM3A6		Max. Occurrence	Maximum Occurrence	Numeric
LDM3A7		Description	Description of entity	Text
LDM3A8		Synonyms	List of Synonyms	Text
LDM3A9		Attribute (Repeating Group)		
		ID	ID of Attribute	ID of existing object
		Indicator	Primary Key	Key Indicator Boolean
		Foreign Key	Relationship IDs	ID of existing relationships
LDM3A10		Relationship (Repeating Group)		
		ID	ID of Relationship	ID of existing relationship
		Optionality	Mandatory / Optional	'MUST BE' / 'MAY BE' / NULL
		Group	Exclusive Group	'EITHER' / 'OR' / NULL
		Link phrase	Description of relationship	Text
		Degree	1:1 or 1:n	'One and only one' / 'One or more'
		Object	Object entity	Name of existing entity

Testing Criteria for the SSADM
Version 4 Tools Conformance Scheme

Attributes | ✓ | Which of the following attributes for each **Entity Description** does the software tool support?

	Name	Description	Validation
LDM3A11	Users - (Repeating Group)		
	User Role	User who have access	Existing User Role
	Access rights	Access rights of user	I,R,M,D,A,ALL
LDM3A12	Owner	Owner of Data	Person/User Role
LDM3A13	Growth per period	Growth rate	Text
LDM3A14	Additional Relationships	Relationships not shown on LDS	Text
LDM3A15	Archive and destruction	Retention factors	Text
LDM3A16	Security measures	Security issues	Text
LDM3A17	State Indicators	SIV ranges/ meanings	Text
LDM3A18	Notes	Comment	Text

Object Representation   None

Quality Criteria | ✓ | Which of the following quality criteria does the software tool enforce?

LDM3QC1	Is the absence of a primary key highlighted? (0,1,3,5,6)
LDM3QC2	Are all relationships on each entity description represented by foreign keys? (1,3,5,6)

Attribute Dependent Tests

Mandatory Relationships   None

Optional Relationships   None

Chapter 10
Logical Data Modelling

Object Representation　　None

Quality Criteria　　None

LDM4　Grouped Domain Description

Each **Grouped Domain Description** has significance as documenting validation rules and formats common to several attributes. (0,1,2,3,4,5,6)

Mandatory Relationships	✓	Does the software tool ensure that each **Grouped Domain Description**
LDM4MR1		describes one and only one **Domain**? (0,1,2,3,4,5,6)
LDM4MR2		belongs to one and only one **Data Catalogue**? (0,1,2,3,4,5,6)

Optional Relationships	✓	Does the software tool allow a **Grouped Domain Description**
LDM4OR1		to reference one or more **User Role**? (3)

Attributes	✓	Which of the following attributes for each **Grouped Domain Description** does the software tool support?		
		Name	**Description**	**Validation**
LDM4A1		Identifier	ID of grouped domain	ID of existing grouped domain‡
LDM4A2		Name	Name of grouped domain	Name of existing grouped domain‡
LDM4A3		Synonyms	List of Synonyms	Text
LDM4A4		Description	Description of grouped domain	Text
LDM4A5		Validation/ Derivation	Validation/ Derivation of grouped domain	Text

203

Testing Criteria for the SSADM
Version 4 Tools Conformance Scheme

Attributes	✓	Which of the following attributes for each **Grouped Domain Description** does the software tool support?		
		Name	Description	Validation
LDM4A6		Default value	Initialisation value	Text
LDM4A7		Null value	Value when not in use	Text
LDM4A8		Logical format	Format of attribute	Numeric, char etc
LDM4A9		Unit of measure	Unit of length	Text
LDM4A10		Logical length	Length of attribute	Text/Numeric
LDM4A11		Length Description	Describing variable lengths	Text
LDM4A12		Users - (Repeating Group)		
		User Role	User who have access	Existing User Role
		Access rights	Access rights of user	I,R,M,D,A,ALL
LDM4A13		Owner	Owner of Data	Person/User Role
LDM4A14		Notes	Comment	Text

Object Representation   None

Quality Criteria	✓	Which of the following quality criteria does the software tool enforce?
LDM4QC1		Does the Grouped Domain Description apply to all the corresponding attributes? (0,1,3,5,6)
LDM4QC2		Does the grouped domain include more than one attribute? (0,1,3,5,6)

Chapter 10
Logical Data Modelling

Attribute Dependent Tests

Mandatory Relationships   None

Optional Relationships   None

Object Representation   None

Quality Criteria   None

LDM5 Logical Data Model

Each **Logical Data Model** has significance as providing a model of the information requirements of all or part of an organisation. The Logical Data Model consists of a Logical Data Structure, Entity Descriptions and Relationship Descriptions. (0,1,3,5) (6)

Mandatory Relationships	✓	Does the software tool ensure that each **Logical Data Model**
LDM5MR1		contains one and only one **Logical Data Structure**? (0,1,3,5)
LDM5MR2		belongs to one and only one **Logical Design**? (5)

Optional Relationships	✓	Does the software tool allow a **Logical Data Model**
LDM5OR1		to augment one or more **Feasibility Option**? (0)

205

Attributes	✓	Which of the following attributes for each **Logical Data Model** does the software tool support?		
		Name	**Description**	**Validation**
LDM5A1		Name	Name of Logical Data Model	Unique ID
LDM5A2		Variant	Variant of Logical	OVERVIEW/ CURRENT ENVIRONMENT /REQUIRED SYSTEM

Object Representation	✓	Does the software tool ensure that each **Logical Data Model** has the following object representation?
LDM5OB1		A **Logical Data Model** is composed of **Logical Data Structure** A set of **Entity Description** A set of **Relationship Descripton**

Quality Criteria	✓	Which of the following quality criteria does the software tool enforce?
LDM5QC1		Are the identifiers of all relationships unique? (0,1,3,5,6)
LDM5QC2		Have all n:m relationships been resolved? (3,5,6)
LDM5QC3		Are all entities of the LDM mapped on the Logical Data Store/Entity Cross-Reference? (1,3)

Chapter 10
Logical Data Modelling

Attribute Dependent Tests

Where attribute: Variant = "CURRENT ENVIRONMENT"

Mandatory Relationships	✓	Does the software tool ensure that each **Logical Data Model**
LDM5ADMR1		belongs to one and only one **Current Services Description**? (1)
LDM5ADMR2		contains *two* or more **Entity Description**? (0,1,3,5)
LDM5ADMR3		contains *two* or more **Relationship Description**? (1,3)

Where attribute: Variant = "REQUIRED SYSTEM"

Mandatory Relationships	✓	Does the software tool ensure that each **Logical Data Model**
LDM5ADMR4		belongs to one and only one **Processing Description**? (3)
LDM5ADMR5		contains *two* or more **Entity Description**? (0,1,3,5)
LDM5ADMR6		contains *two* or more **Relationship Description**? (1,3)
LDM5ADMR7		belongs to one and only one **Physical Process Description**? (6)
LDM5ADMR8		belongs to one and only one **Logical Design**? (5)

Optional Relationships   None

Object Representation   None

Testing Criteria for the SSADM
Version 4 Tools Conformance Scheme

Where attribute: Variant = "CURRENT ENVIRONMENT"

Quality Criteria	✓	Which of the following quality criteria does the software tool enforce?
LDM5ADQC1		Are all entities on the Logical Data Structure described in the Entity Descriptions? (1,3,5)
LDM5ADQC2		Are all the relationships on the Logical Data Structure described in the Relationship Descriptions? (1,3,5)

Where attribute: Variant = "REQUIRED SYSTEM"

Quality Criteria	✓	Which of the following quality criteria does the software tool enforce?
LDM5ADQC3		Are all entities on the Logical Data Structure described in the Entity Descriptions? (1,3,5)
LDM5ADQC4		Are all the relationships on the Logical Data Structure described in the Relationship Descriptions? (1,3,5)

Chapter 10
Logical Data Modelling

LDM6 Logical Data Structure

Each **Logical Data Structure** has significance as a diagrammatic representation of the information needs of an organisation in the form of entities and the important business relationships between them. (0,1,3) (2)

Mandatory Relationships	✓	Does the software tool ensure that each **Logical Data Structure**
LDM6MR1		belongs to one and only one **Logical Data Model**? (0,1,3) OR documents one and only one **Selected Business System Option**? (2) OR documents one and only one **Business System Option**? (2) OR documents one and only one **Feasibility Report**? (0)
LDM6MR2		contains one or more **Entity Type**? (0,1,3)
LDM6MR3		contains one or more **Relationship Type**? (0,1,3)

Optional Relationships   None

Attributes	✓	Which of the following attributes for each **Logical Data Structure** does the software tool support?		
		Name	Description	Validation
LDM6A1		Name	Name of Diagram	Unique ID

Object Representation	✓	Does the software tool ensure that each **Logical Data Structure** has the following object representation?

LDM6OB1		A **Logical Data Structure** is composed of
		    Entity Type
		    Relationship Type

Quality Criteria   None

209

Testing Criteria for the SSADM
Version 4 Tools Conformance Scheme

Attribute Dependent Tests

Mandatory Relationships None

Optional Relationships None

Object Representation None

Quality Criteria None

LDM7 Relationship Description

Each **Relationship Description** has significance as documenting the details of a relationship between two entities on the Logical Data Structure. (1,3)

Mandatory Relationships	✓	Does the software tool ensure that each **Relationship Description**
LDM7MR1		describes one direction of one and only one **Relationship Type**? (1,3)
LDM7MR2		describes one and only one **Relationship End**? (1,3)
LDM7MR3		references *two* and only *two* **Entity Type**? (1,3)
LDM7MR4		belongs to one and only one **Logical Data Model**? (1,3)

Optional Relationships	✓	Does the software tool allow a **Relationship Description**
LDM7OR1		to reference one or more **User Role**? (3)

Chapter 10
Logical Data Modelling

Attributes	✓	Which of the following attributes for each **Relationship Description** does the software tool support?		
		Name	Description	Validation
LDM7A1		Variant	Name of Logical Data Model variant	Text
LDM7A2		Identifier	ID of subject entity	ID of existing entity
LDM7A3		Name	Name of subject entity	Name of existing entity
LDM7A4		Optionality	Optionality of relationship	OPTIONAL/ MANDATORY
LDM7A5		Percentage	Percentage of Optionality	Numeric
LDM7A6		Link Phrase	Link Phrase for relationship	Text‡
LDM7A7		Description	Description of relationship	Text
LDM7A8		Alternative Phrase	Alternative Link Phrase	Text
LDM7A9		Object entity name	Name of object entity	Name of existing entity
LDM7A10		Object entity Identifier	ID of object entity	ID of existing entity
LDM7A11		Cardinality	1:1 or 1:n	1:1/1:n
LDM7A12		Minimum	Minimum cardinality	Numeric
LDM7A13		Average	Average cardinality	Numeric
LDM7A14		Maximum	Maximum cardinality	Numeric
LDM7A15		Cardinality description	Description of cardinality	Text Description
LDM7A16		Growth	Growth per period	Text
LDM7A17		Properties	Additional properties	Text

211

Testing Criteria for the SSADM
Version 4 Tools Conformance Scheme

Attributes	✓	Which of the following attributes for each **Relationship Description** does the software tool support?		
		Name	Description	Validation
LDM7A18		Users - (Repeating Group)		
		User Role	User who have access	Existing User Role
		Access rights	Access rights of user	I,R,M,D,A,ALL
LDM7A19		Owner	Owner of Data	Person/User Role
LDM7A20		Notes	Comment	Text

Object Representation None

Quality Criteria None

Attribute Dependent Tests

Mandatory Relationships None

Optional Relationships None

Object Representation None

Quality Criteria None

Chapter 10
Logical Data Modelling

LDM51 Entity Type

Each **Entity Type** has significance as a kind or sort of object or concept, either concrete or abstract, which is of importance to the environment under investigation. (0,1,3,5)

Mandatory Relationships	✓	Does the software tool ensure that each **Entity Type**
LDM51MR1		is described by one and only one **Entity Description**? (0,1,3,5)
LDM51MR2		is part of one and only one **Logical Data Structure**? (0,1,3)
LDM51MR3		is the subject reference to one or more **Relationship Description**? (1,3)
LDM51MR4		is the object reference to one or more **Relationship Description**? (1,3)
LDM51MR5		is described by one and only one **Entity Life History**? (3)
LDM51MR6		is documented by one and only one **ELH Node**? (3)
LDM51MR7		is referenced by one and only one **Logical Data Store/Entity Cross-Reference Detail**? (1,3)
LDM51MR8		is referenced by one or more **Process/Entity Matrix Entry**? (1)
LDM51MR9		is referenced by one or more **Event/Entity Matrix Entry**? (3)

Optional Relationships	✓	Does the software tool allow an **Entity Type**
LDM51OR1		to be the context for one or more **Exclusive Relationship Group**? (0,1,3)
LDM51OR2		to have its occurrences documented by one or more **EAP Node**? (3)
LDM51OR3		to be represented by one and only one **Relation**? (3)

Testing Criteria for the SSADM
Version 4 Tools Conformance Scheme

Attributes	✓	Which of the following attributes for each **Entity Type** does the software tool support?		
		Name	**Description**	**Validation**
LDM51A1		Identifier	ID of entity type	Unique ID
LDM51A2		Name	Name of entity type	Unique Name

Object Representation	✓	Does the software tool ensure that each **Entity Type** has the following object representation?
LDM51OB1		Entity Name / Incomplete Entity Name

Quality Criteria   None

Attribute Dependent Tests

Mandatory Relationships   None

Optional Relationships   None

Object Representation   None

Quality Criteria   None

Chapter 10
Logical Data Modelling

LDM52 Relationship Type

Each **Relationship Type** has significance as a type of association between entities of two types or the same type. (0,1,3)

Mandatory Relationships	✓	Does the software tool ensure that each **Relationship Type**
LDM52MR1		is described by *two* and only *two* **Relationship Description**? (1,3)
LDM52MR2		is represented by one and only one **Logical Data Structure**? (0,1,3)
LDM52MR3		contains *two* and only *two* **Relationship End**? (0,1,3)

Optional Relationships   None

Attributes	✓	Which of the following attributes for each **Relationship Type** does the software tool support?		
		Name	Description	Validation
LDM52A1		Identifier (Group)		
		Master	Master entity	Existing master entity
		Detail	Detail entity	Existing detail entity
		Type No	Type occurrence	Cardinal

215

Testing Criteria for the SSADM Version 4 Tools Conformance Scheme

Object Representation	✓	Does the software tool ensure that each **Relationship Type** has the following object representation?
LDM52OB1		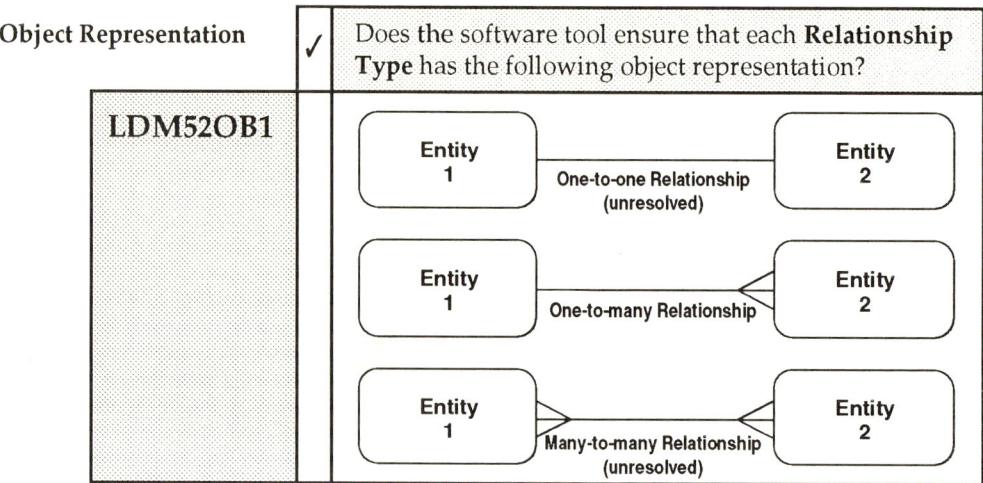

Quality Criteria   None

Attribute Dependent Tests

Where Attribute: Master = Attribute: Detail

Mandatory Relationships	✓	Does the software tool ensure that each **Relationship Type**
LDM52ADMR1		is referenced by one and only one **Entity Description**? (0,1,3)

Where Attribute: Master NOT = Attribute: Detail

Mandatory Relationships	✓	Does the software tool ensure that each **Relationship Type**
LDM52ADMR1		is referenced by *two* and only *two* **Entity Description**? (0,1,3)

Optional Relationships   None

Chapter 10
Logical Data Modelling

Where Attribute: Master = Attribute: Detail

Object Representation	✓	Does the software tool ensure that each **Relationship Type** has the following object representation?
LDM52ADOB1		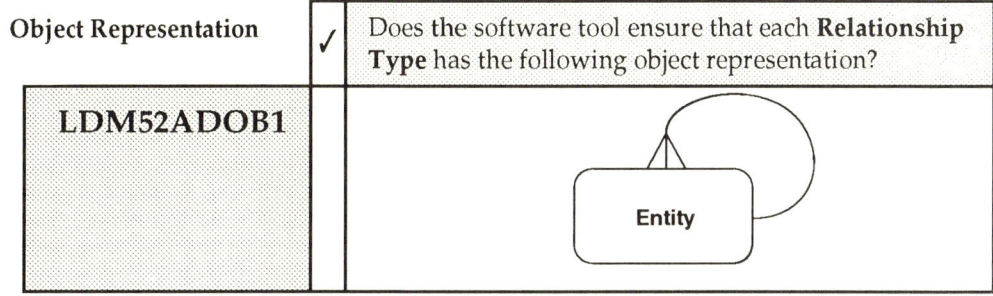

Quality Criteria   None

LDM53 Relationship End

Each **Relationship End** has significance as describing the two ends of a relationship type (i.e. their optionality and degree).

The optionality can be optional or mandatory and the degree can be one of the following:

- zero or one (optional)
- zero, one or more (optional)
- exactly one (mandatory)
- at least one or more (mandatory).

(0,1,3)

Mandatory Relationships	✓	Does the software tool ensure that each **Relationship End**
LDM53MR1		is part of one and only one **Relationship Type**? (0,1,3)
LDM53MR2		is described by one and only one **Relationship Description**? (1,3)

Testing Criteria for the SSADM
Version 4 Tools Conformance Scheme

Optional Relationships	✓	Does the software tool allow a **Relationship End**		
LDM53OR1		to belong to one and only one **Exclusive Relationship Group**? (0,1,3)		
Attributes	✓	Which of the following attributes for each **Relationship End** does the software tool support?		
		Name	Description	Validation
LDM53A1		Identifier	Relationship Type ID + Entity Type ID	ID of existing relationship type and entity type
LDM53A2		Optionality	Optionality of relationship end	OPTIONAL/ MANDATORY
LDM53A3		Degree	Degree of relationship end	ONE and ONLY ONE / ONE OR MORE
LDM53A4		Link Phrase	Relationship end link phrase	Text

Object Representation   None

Quality Criteria   None

Attribute Dependent Tests

Mandatory Relationships   None

Optional Relationships   None

Chapter 10
Logical Data Modelling

Where Attribute: Optionality = "OPTIONAL"

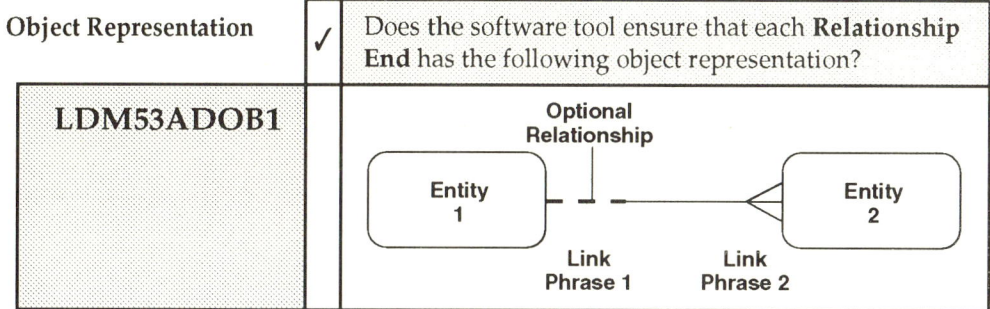

Where Attribute: Optionality = "MANDATORY"

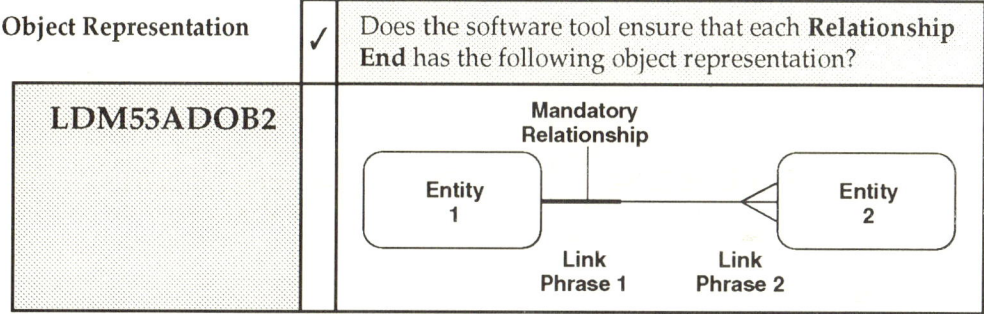

Where Attribute: Degree = "ONE AND ONLY ONE"

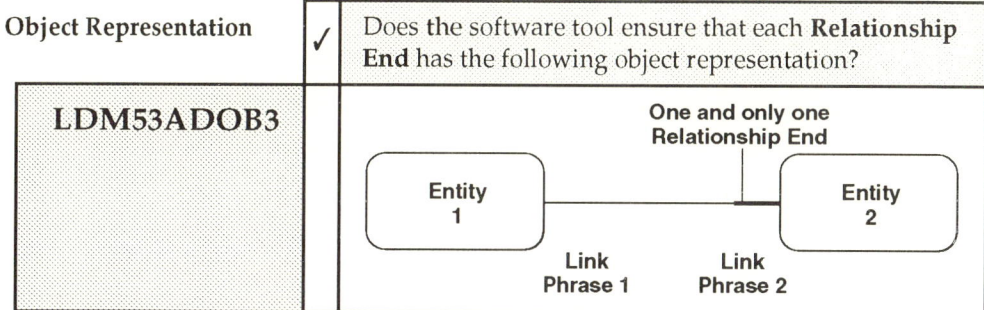

Where Attribute: Degree = "ONE OR MORE"

Object Representation	✓	Does the software tool ensure that each **Relationship End** has the following object representation?
LDM53ADOB4		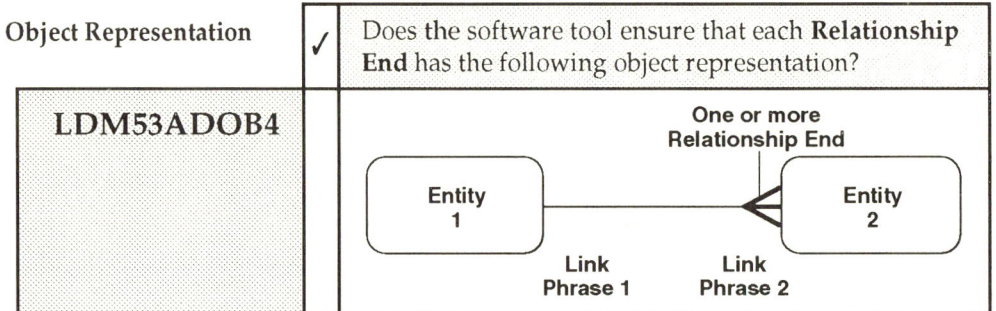

Quality Criteria   None

LDM54 Domain

Each **Domain** (to include grouped domain) has significance as a set of permissible values. A domain defines the possible values of a data type. A domain may consist of the cross product of two or more domains; this is termed a grouped domain. (0,1,2,3,4,5,6)

Mandatory Relationships   None

Optional Relationships   None

Attributes	✓	Which of the following attributes for each **Domain (to include grouped domain)** does the software tool support?		
		Name	Description	Validation
LDM54A1		Identifier	Domain ID	Unique ID
LDM54A2		Name	Name of domain	Text
LDM54A3		Type	Type of domain	ELEMENTARY /COMPOSITE

Object Representation   None

Quality Criteria   None

Chapter 10
Logical Data Modelling

Attribute Dependent Tests

Where attribute: Type = "ELEMENTARY"

Mandatory Relationships	✓	Does the software tool ensure that each **Domain**
LDM54ADMR1		is associated with one or more **Attribute Type**? (0,1,2,3,4,5,6)

Where attribute: Type = "COMPOSITE"

Mandatory Relationships	✓	Does the software tool ensure that each **Domain**
LDM54ADMR2		is part of one and only one **Grouped Domain Description**? (0,1,3,4,5,6)
LDM54ADMR3		is associated with *two* or more **Attribute Type**? (0,1,3,4,5,6)

Optional Relationships   None

Object Representation   None

Quality Criteria   None

221

LDM55 Attribute Type

Each **Attribute Type** has significance as a class of characteristics that describe the same characteristic of all entities of a type. (0,1,3,4,5,6)

Mandatory Relationships	✓	Does the software tool ensure that each **Attribute Type**
LDM55MR1		is described in one and only one **Attribute/Data Item Description**? (0,1,3,4,5,6)
LDM55MR2		is referenced by one or more **Entity Description**? (0,1,3,5)
LDM55MR3		is contained within one or more **Domain**? (0,1,3,4,5,6)

Optional Relationships	✓	Does the software tool allow an **Attribute Type**
LDM55OR1		to be used by one or more **I/O Description**? (1,3)
LDM55OR2		to be the source of input to one or more **Effect Correspondence Diagram**? (1,3)
LDM55OR3		to be part of one or more **Enquiry Trigger**? (3)
LDM55OR4		to be part of one or more **I/O Structure Element**? (3)
LDM55OR5		to be part of one or more **Relation**? (3)
LDM55OR6		to be part of one or more **Simple Key**? (3)
LDM55OR7		to be part of one or more **Composite Key**? (3)
LDM55OR8		to be part of one or more **Dialogue Element**? (3)

Chapter 10
Logical Data Modelling

Attributes	✓	Which of the following attributes for each **Attribute Type** does the software tool support?		
		Name	Description	Validation
LDM55A1		Identifier	ID of attribute	Unique ID
LDM55A2		Name	Name of attribute	Unique

Object Representation   None

Quality Criteria   None

Attribute Dependent Tests

Mandatory Relationships   None

Optional Relationships   None

Object Representation   None

Quality Criteria   None

Testing Criteria for the SSADM
Version 4 Tools Conformance Scheme

LDM56 Exclusive Relationship Group

Each **Exclusive Relationship Group** has significance when the participation of an entity occurrence in one relationship precludes its participation in one or more other relationships. (0,1,3)

Mandatory Relationships	✓	Does the software tool ensure that each **Exclusive Relationship Group**
LDM56MR1		is for one and only one **Entity Type**? (0,1,3)
LDM56MR2		includes *two* or more **Relationship End**? (0,1,3)

Optional Relationships None

Attributes	✓	Which of the following attributes for each **Attribute Type** does the software tool support?		
		Name	Description	Validation
LDM56A1		Identifier	All relationship end IDs within the group	Existing relationship ends

Chapter 10
Logical Data Modelling

Object Representation	✓	Does the software tool ensure that each **Exclusive Relationship Group** has the following object representation?
LDM56OB1		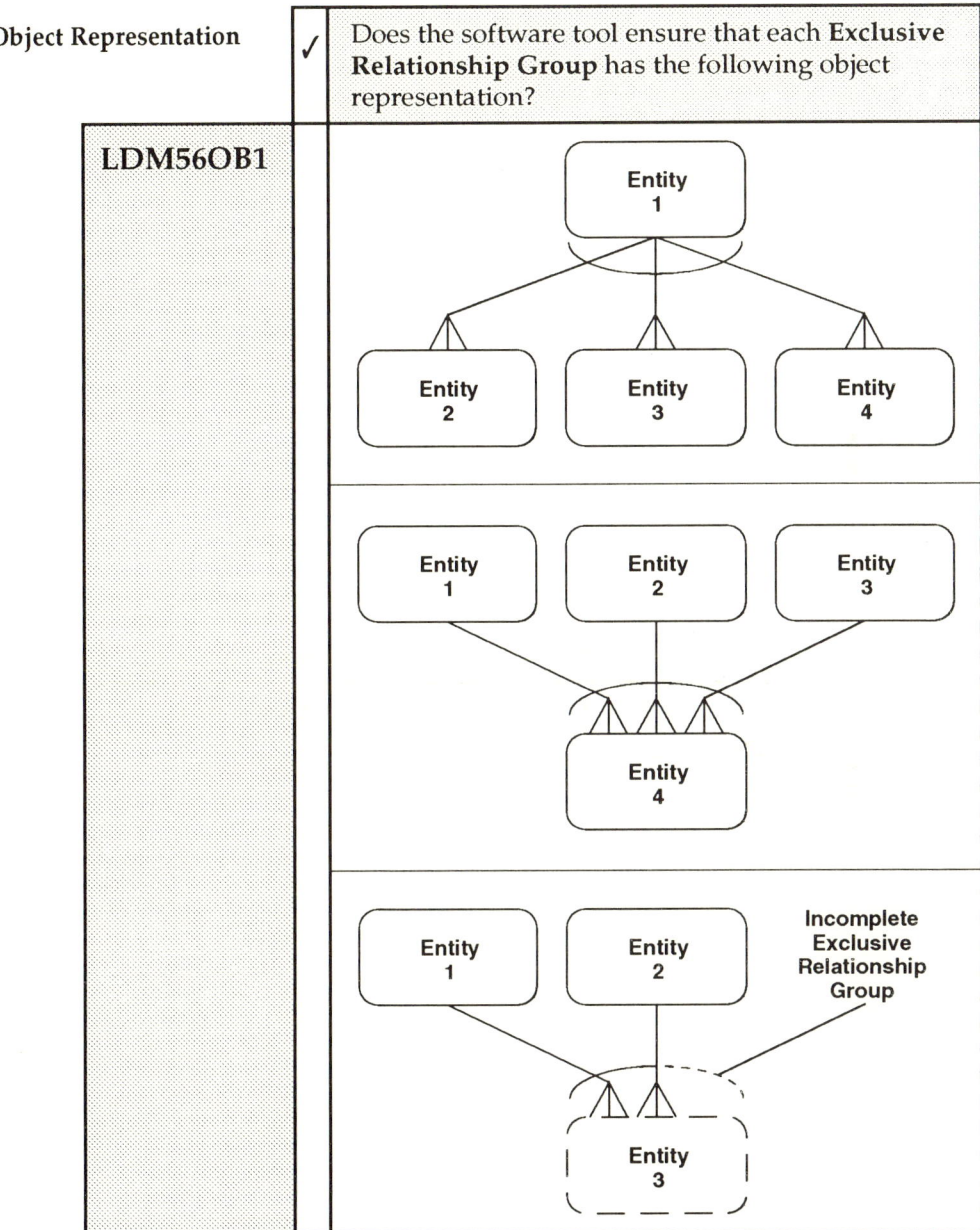

225

Testing Criteria for the SSADM
Version 4 Tools Conformance Scheme

Quality Criteria	✓	Which of the following quality criteria does the software tool enforce?
LDM56QC1		Do the relationship ends in an exclusive relationship group have the same optionality? (0,1,3)
LDM56QC2		Are the relationship ends in an exclusive relationship group associated with the same entity type? (0,1,3)

Attribute Dependent Tests

Mandatory Relationships   None

Optional Relationships   None

Object Representation   None

Quality Criteria   None

11 Logical Database Process Design

This chapter contains tests for the following products and concepts:

Products

LDP1	Enquiry Process Model	228
LDP2	Logical Process Model	229
LDP3	Update Process Model	230

Concepts

LDP51	Logical Database Process	232
LDP52	Logical Database Process Node	233
LDP53	Logical Database Process Operation	240
LDP54	Condition	242

LDP1 Enquiry Process Model

Each **Enquiry Process Model** has significance as a structure diagram for an enquiry processing requirement and the associated Operations List. The structure is based on the Enquiry Access Path. (3) (5)

Mandatory Relationships	✓	Does the software tool ensure that each **Enquiry Process Model**
LDP1MR1		belongs to one and only one **Logical Process Model**? (5)
LDP1MR2		consists of one and only one **Logical Database Process**? (3)
LDP1MR3		contains one or more **Logical Database Process Operation**? (3)
LDP1MR4		is based on one and only one **Enquiry Access Path**? (3)

Optional Relationships   None

Attributes	✓	Which of the following attributes for each **Enquiry Process Model** does the software tool support?		
		Name	Description	Validation
LDP1A1		Identifier	Enquiry Name	Existing enquiry function

Object Representation	✓	Does the software tool ensure that each **Enquiry Process Model** has the following object representation?
LDP1OB1		An **Enquiry Process Model** consists of **Logical Database Process** **Logical Database Process Operation**

Quality Criteria   None

Chapter 11
Logical Database Process Design

Attribute Dependent Tests

Object Representation None

Quality Criteria None

LDP2 Logical Process Model

Each **Logical Process Model** has significance as packaging all processing details within the Logical Design. (5)

Mandatory Relationships	✓	Does the software tool ensure that each **Logical Process Model**
LDP2MR1		contains one and only one **Dialogues**? (5)
LDP2MR2		contains one or more **Effect Correspondence Diagram**? (5)
LDP2MR3		contains one or more **Enquiry Process Model**? (5)
LDP2MR4		contains one and only one **Function Definitions**? (5)
LDP2MR5		contains one or more **Update Process Model**? (5)
LDP2MR6		belongs to one and only one **Logical Design**? (5)

Optional Relationships None

Attributes	✓	Which of the following attributes for each **Logical Process Model** does the software tool support?		
		Name	Description	Validation
LDP2A1		Name	Name of model	Unique ID

229

Testing Criteria for the SSADM
Version 4 Tools Conformance Scheme

Object Representation	✓	Does the software tool ensure that each **Logical Process Model** has the following object representation?

LDP2OB1		A **Logical Process Model** consists of
		    Dialogues
		    Effect Correspondence Diagram
		    Enquiry Process Model
		    Function Definitions
		    Update Process Model

Quality Criteria	✓	Which of the following quality criteria does the software tool enforce?
LDP2QC1		Do the Function Definitions include only those I/O Structures which have not been superseded by the Enquiry or Update Process models? (5)
LDP2QC2		Are all the Effect Correspondence Diagrams present? (5)

Attribute Dependent Tests

Object Representation   one

Quality Criteria   None

LDP3   Update Process Model

Each **Update Process Model** has significance as a structure diagram for the update (event) processing requirement and the associated Operations List. This is based on the Entity Life Histories, which provide a data-oriented view of the system, and the associated Effect Correspondence Diagrams, which provide an event-oriented or process-oriented view of the system. (5)

Chapter 11
Logical Database Process Design

Mandatory Relationships	✓	Does the software tool ensure that each **Update Process Model**
LDP3MR1		is based on one and only one **Effect Correspondence Diagram**? (5)
LDP3MR2		is based on one or more **Entity Life History**? (5)
LDP3MR3		belongs to one and only one **Logical Process Model**? (5)
LDP3MR4		consists of one and only one **Logical Database Process**? (5)
LDP3MR5		contains one or more **Logical Database Process Operation**? (5)

Optional Relationships   None

Attributes		✓	Which of the following attributes for each **Update Process Model** does the software tool support?	
		Name	Description	Validation
LDP3A1		Identifier	Event name	Existing event

Object Representation	✓	Does the software tool ensure that each **Update Process Model** has the following object representation?

LDP3OB1		An **Update Process Model** consists of
		    Logical Database Process
		    Logical Database Process Operation

Quality Criteria   None

Attribute Dependent Tests

Object Representation   None

Quality Criteria   None

LDP51 Logical Database Process

Each **Logical Database Process** has significance as a sequential structure of nodes that describe a particular named unit of processing that forms part of a system. (3,5)

Mandatory Relationships	✓	Does the software tool ensure that each **Logical Database Process**
LDP51MR1		contains one or more **Logical Database Process Node**? (3,5)
LDP51MR2		is documented by one and only one **Logical Database Process Node**? (3,5)

Optional Relationships   None

Attributes	✓	Which of the following attributes for each **Logical Database Process** does the software tool support?		
		Name	Description	Validation
LDP51A1		Identifier	Database Process	Unique
LDP51A2		Type	Process Type	ENQUIRY/ UPDATE

Object Representation	✓	Does the software tool ensure that each **Logical Database Process** has the following object representation?
LDP51OB1		A **Logical Database Process** consists of **Logical Database Process Node**

Quality Criteria   None

Chapter 11
Logical Database Process Design

Attribute Dependent Tests

Where attribute: Type = "ENQUIRY"

Mandatory Relationships	✓	Does the software tool ensure that each **Logical Database Process**
LDP51ADMR1		belongs to one and only one **Enquiry Process Model**? (3)

Where attribute: Type = "UPDATE"

Mandatory Relationships	✓	Does the software tool ensure that each **Logical Database Process**
LDP51ADMR2		belongs to one and only one **Update Process Model**? (5)

Object Representation   None

Quality Criteria   None

LDP52 Logical Database Process Node

Each **Logical Database Process Node** has significance as a node on a Logical Database Process. Each node must be one of the following types:

- a root node
- an intermediate node
- a leaf node.

Each node must have one of the following structures:

- a sequence node
- a selection node
- an iteration node
- an operation node. (3,5)

233

Testing Criteria for the SSADM
Version 4 Tools Conformance Scheme

Mandatory Relationships	✓	Does the software tool ensure that each **Logical Database Process Node**
LDP52MR1		is part of one and only one **Logical Database Process**? (3,5)

Optional Relationships	✓	Does the software tool allow a **Logical Database Process Node**
LDP52OR1		to be the child of one and only one **Logical Database Process Node**? (3,5)
LDP52OR2		to be the parent of one or more **Logical Database Process Node**? (3,5)
LDP52OR3		to document one and only one **Condition**? (3,5)

Attributes		✓	Which of the following attributes for each **Logical Database Process Node** does the software tool support?		
			Name	Description	Validation
LDP52A1			Name	Name of node	Text
LDP52A2			Type	Type of node	ROOT/ INTERMEDIATE /LEAF
LDP52A3			Structure	Structure type of node	SEQUENCE/ SELECTION/ ITERATION/ OPERATION

Object Representation   None

Quality Criteria   None

Chapter 11
Logical Database Process Design

Attribute Dependent Tests

Where attribute: Type = "ROOT"

Mandatory Relationships	✓	Does the software tool ensure that each **Logical Database Process Node**
LDP52ADMR1		is in one-to-one correspondence with one and only one **Logical Database Process**? (3,5)
LDP52ADMR2		is the parent of one or more **Logical Database Process Node**? (3,5)

Where attribute: Type = "INTERMEDIATE"

Mandatory Relationships	✓	Does the software tool ensure that each **Logical Database Process Node**
LDP52ADMR3		is the child of one and only one **Logical Database Process Node**? (3,5)
LDP52ADMR4		is the parent of one or more **Logical Database Process Node**? (3,5)

Where attribute: Type = "LEAF"

Mandatory Relationships	✓	Does the software tool ensure that each **Logical Database Process Node**
LDP52ADMR5		is the child of one and only one **Logical Database Process Node**? (3,5)

Testing Criteria for the SSADM
Version 4 Tools Conformance Scheme

Where attribute: Type = "SEQUENCE"

Mandatory Relationships	✓	Does the software tool ensure that each **Logical Database Process Node**
LDP52ADMR6		is the parent of *two* or more **Logical Database Process Node**? (3,5)

Where attribute: Type = "SELECTION"

Mandatory Relationships	✓	Does the software tool ensure that each **Logical Database Process Node**
LDP52ADMR7		is the parent of *two* or more **Logical Database Process Node**? (3,5)

Where attribute: Type = "ITERATION"

Mandatory Relationships	✓	Does the software tool ensure that each **Logical Database Process Node**
LDP52ADMR8		is the parent of one and only one **Logical Database Process Node**? (3,5)

Where attribute: Type = "OPERATION"

Mandatory Relationships	✓	Does the software tool ensure that each **Logical Database Process Node**
LDP52ADMR9		represents one and only one **Logical Database Process Operation**? (3,5)

Chapter 11
Logical Database Process Design

Where attribute: Type = "ROOT"

Object Representation	✓	Does the software tool ensure that each **Logical Database Process Node** has the following object representation for the given attribute value?
LDP52ADOB1		Logical Database Process Name

Where attribute: Type = "SEQUENCE"

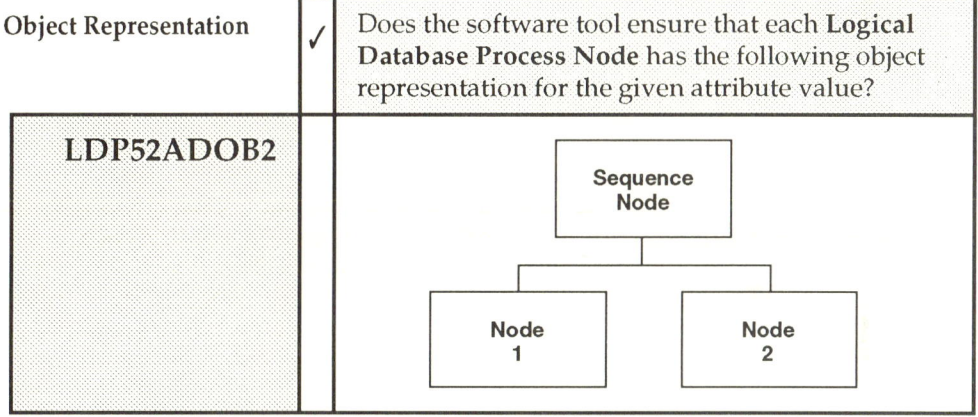

Where attribute: Type = "SELECTION"

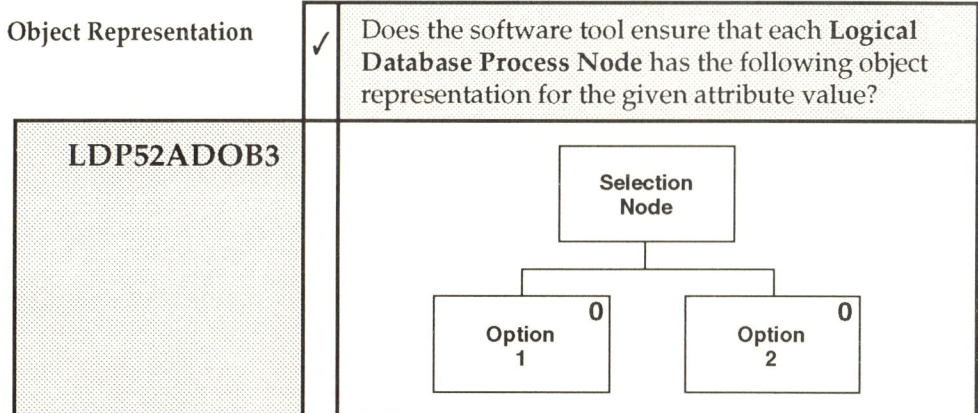

237

Where attribute: Type = "ITERATION"

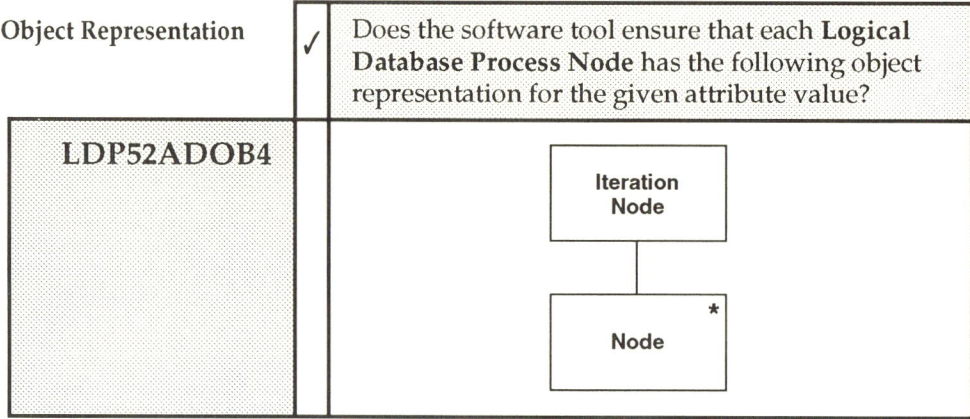

Object Representation	✓	Does the software tool ensure that each **Logical Database Process Node** has the following object representation for the given attribute value?
LDP52ADOB4		

Where attribute: Type = "OPERATION"

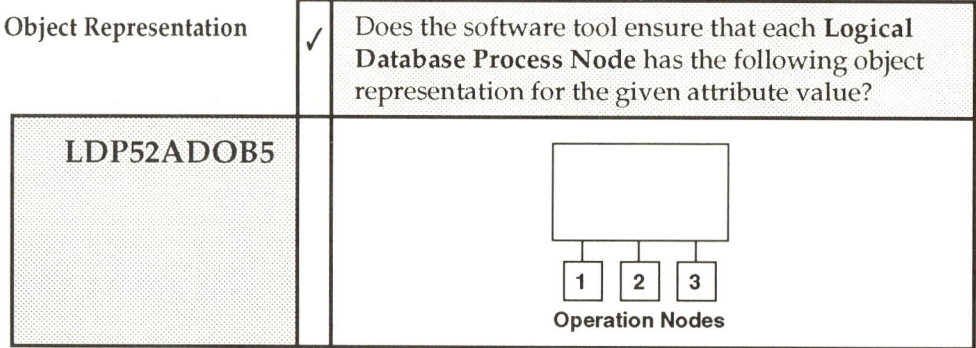

Object Representation	✓	Does the software tool ensure that each **Logical Database Process Node** has the following object representation for the given attribute value?
LDP52ADOB5		

Where attribute: Type = "ROOT"

Quality Criteria	✓	Which of the following quality criteria does the software tool enforce?
LDP52ADQC1		Attribute: Name = An existing Logical Database Process Name (3,5)

Chapter 11
Logical Database Process Design

Where attribute: Type = "LEAF"

Quality Criteria	✓	Which of the following quality criteria does the software tool enforce?
LDP52ADQC2		Attribute: Structure = "OPERATION" (3,5)

Where attribute: Type = "SELECTION"

Quality Criteria	✓	Which of the following quality criteria does the software tool enforce?
LDP52ADQC3		The children nodes must have associated conditions. (3,5)

Where attribute: Type = "ITERATION"

Quality Criteria	✓	Which of the following quality criteria does the software tool enforce?
LDP52ADQC4		Attribute: Type = "INTERMEDIATE" (3,5) The child node must have an associated condition. (3,5)

Where attribute: Type = "OPERATION"

Quality Criteria	✓	Which of the following quality criteria does the software tool enforce?
LDP52ADQC5		Where attribute: Structure = "OPERATION" Attribute: Name = A Cardinal (3,5) Attribute: Type = "LEAF" (3,5) The **Logical Database Process Node** must have no children (3,5) The parent of the **Logical Database Process Node** Attribute: Type = "INTERMEDIATE". (3,5)

LDP53 Logical Database Process Operation

Each **Logical Database Process Operation** has significance as a discrete component of processing performed by a Logical Database Process. (3,5)

Mandatory Relationships	✓	Does the software tool ensure that each **Logical Database Process Operation**
LDP53MR1		is documented by one or more **Logical Database Process Node**? (3,5)

Optional Relationships None

Attributes		✓	Which of the following attributes for each **Logical Database Process Operation** does the software tool support?		
			Name	Description	Validation
	LDP53A1		Identifier	Operation number	Cardinal, unique to model
	LDP53A2		Description	Description of Operation	Text
	LDP53A3		Type	Enquiry or update	'E'/'U'
	LDP53A4		Processing	Type of operation	READ <Entity type> BY <Keys> /DEFINE SET OF <Entity type> MATCHING INPUT DATA/ READ NEXT <Entity type> IN SET/ READ NEXT <Detail> OF <Master> [VIA <Relationship>] /READ <Master> OF <Detail> [VIA <Relationship>]

Chapter 11
Logical Database Process Design

Attributes	✓	Which of the following attributes for each **Logical Database Process Operation** does the software tool support?		
		Name	Description	Validation
(LDP53A4 contd)		(Processing contd)	(Type of operation contd)	/INVOKE <Common Process> /FAIL IF SI OF <Entity> outside <SI range>/Any ELH Operation

Object Representation	✓	Does the software tool ensure that each **Logical Database Process Operation** has the following object representation?
LDP53OB1		☐ ┌─┬─┬─┐ │1│2│3│ └─┴─┴─┘ **Operation Nodes** 1. Text associated with Operation 1 2. Text associated with Operation 2 ......

Quality Criteria	✓	Which of the following quality criteria does the software tool enforce?
LDP53QC1		Are all "Read Next <entity> in Set" operations precededby a "Define Set of <entity> matching input data" opereation? (3,5)
LDP53QC2		Are all the operations used at least once? (3,5)

Attribute Dependent Tests

Where attribute: Type = "U"

Mandatory Relationships	✓	Does the software tool ensure that each **Logical Database Process Operation**
LDP53ADMR1		belongs to one and only one **Update Process Model**? (3,5)

Where attribute: Type = "E"

Mandatory Relationships	✓	Does the software tool ensure that each **Logical Database Process Operation**
LDP53ADMR2		belongs to one and only one **Enquiry Process Model**? (3,5)

Object Representation   None

Where attribute: Type = "U"

Quality Criteria	✓	Which of the following quality criteria does the software tool enforce?
LDP53ADQC1		Attribute: Processing = Any ELH Operation

LDP54 Condition

Each **Condition** has significance as a boolean expression that can be evaluated to true or false. A condition shall be attached to each option of a selection and each iteration node by the end of logical database process design. (3,5)

Chapter 11
Logical Database Process Design

Mandatory Relationships	✓	Does the software tool ensure that each **Condition**
LDP54MR1		is documented by one and only one **Logical Database Process Node**? (3,5)

Optional Relationships   None

Attributes		✓	Which of the following attributes for each **Condition** does the software tool support?
		Name	**Description**	**Validation**
LDP54A1		Type	Type of condition	SELECTION/ITERATION
LDP54A2		Description	Description of condition	IF <condition>/WHILE <condition>

Object Representation   None

Quality Criteria   None

Attribute Dependent Tests

Where attribute: Type = "SELECTION"

Object Representation	✓	Does the software tool ensure that each **Condition** has the following object representation for the given attribute value?
LDP54ADOB1		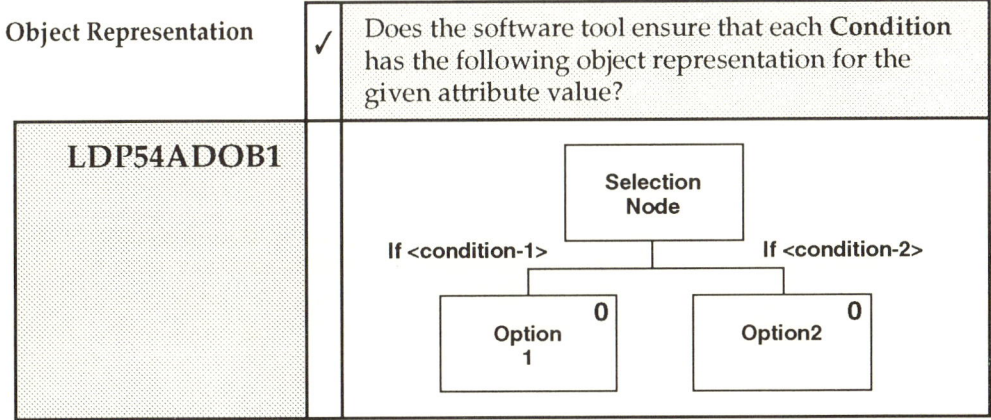

243

Where attribute: Type = "ITERATION"

Object Representation	✓	Does the software tool ensure that each **Condition** has the following object representation for the given attribute value?
LDP54ADOB2		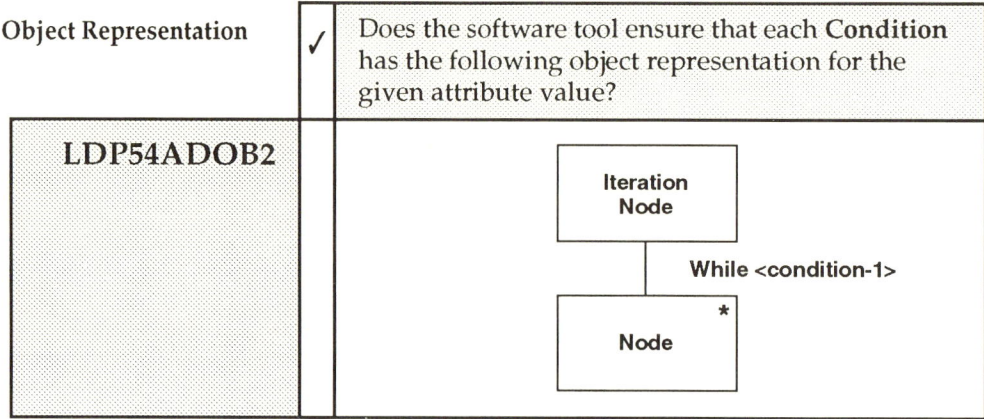

Where attribute: Type = "SELECTION"

Quality Criteria	✓	Which of the following quality criteria does the software tool enforce?
LDP54ADQC1		Attribute: Description = "IF <condition>"

Where attribute: Type = "ITERATION"

Quality Criteria	✓	Which of the following quality criteria does the software tool enforce?
LDP54ADQC2		Attribute: Description = "WHILE <condition>"

Chapter 12
Processing Specification

12 Processing Specification

This chapter contains tests for the following products and concepts:

Products

PSN1	Processing Specification	246
PSN2	Logical Design	248
PSN3	Logical System Specification	250
PSN4	Physical System Specification	251

Testing Criteria for the SSADM
Version 4 Tools Conformance Scheme

PSN1 Processing Specification

Each **Processing Specification** has significance as specifying the processing requirements such that possible solutions can be identified. (3)

Mandatory Relationships | ✓ | Does the software tool ensure that each **Processing Specification**

PSN1MR1	belongs to one and only one **Requirements Specification**? (3)
PSN1MR2	contains one and only one **User Role/Function Matrix**? (3)
PSN1MR3	contains one and only one **Function Definitions**? (3)
PSN1MR4	contains one and only one **Logical Data Model**? (3)
PSN1MR5	contains one or more **Entity Life History**? (3)
PSN1MR6	contains one or more **Effect Correspondence Diagram**? (3)

Optional Relationships   None

Attributes | ✓ | Which of the following attributes for each **Processing Specification** does the software tool support?

	Name	Description	Validation
PSN1A1	Identifier	ID of processing specification	Unique

Object Representation | ✓ | Does the software tool ensure that each **Processing Specification** has the following object representation?

PSN1OB1	A **Processing Specification** consists of
	    User Role/Function Matrix
	    Function Definitions
	    Logical Data Model
	    Entity Life History
	    Effect Correspondence Diagram

Chapter 12
Processing Specification

Quality Criteria	✓	Which of the following quality criteria does the software tool enforce?
PSN1QC1		Do all the items described in operations for an ELH appear as attributes for that entity on the Data Catalogue? (3)
PSN1QC2		Does every event in the Entity Life Histories appear in the appropriate Effect Correspondence Diagrams? (3)
PSN1QC3		Have all events identified as a result of entity life history analysis been allocated to at least one function? (3)
PSN1QC4		Has an Enquiry Access Path been defined for each enquiry function? (3)
PSN1QC5		Does the event data for an ECD exist as input data on all the functions for the event? (3)
PSN1QC6		Are all input data items represented as event data on the ECD for the corresponding event? (3)
PSN1QC7		Is the notation used to highlight entity roles different from that used to highlight effect qualifiers? (3)
PSN1QC8		Is the notation used to highlight entity roles and effect qualifiers consistent between ELHs and ECDs? (3)

Attribute Dependent Tests

Mandatory Relationships None

Optional Relationships None

Object Representation None

Quality Criteria None

Testing Criteria for the SSADM
Version 4 Tools Conformance Scheme

PSN2 Logical Design

Each **Logical Design** has significance as the stage product from Stage 5: Logical design. It packages the logical view of processing with Required System Logical Data Model and the Requirements Catalogue. (5)

Mandatory Relationships	✓	Does the software tool ensure that each **Logical Design**
PSN2MR1		belongs to one and only one **Logical System Specification**? (5)
PSN2MR2		contains one or more **Command Structure**? (5)
PSN2MR3		contains one and only one **Data Catalogue**? (5)
PSN2MR4		contains one and only one **Logical Process Model**? (5)
PSN2MR5		contains one or more **Menu Structure**? (5)
PSN2MR6		contains one and only one **Logical Data Model**? (5)
PSN2MR7		contains one and only one **Requirements Catalogue**? (5)

Optional Relationships   None

Attributes	✓	Which of the following attributes for each **Logical Design** does the software tool support?	
		Name	Description	Validation
PSN2A1		Identifier	ID of Logical Design	Unique

Object Representation	✓	Does the software tool ensure that each **Logical Design** has the following object representation?

PSN2OB1		A **Logical Design** consists of
		    A set of **Command Structure**
		    Data Catalogue
		    Logical Process Model
		    A set of **Menu Structure**
		    Logical Data Model
		    Requirements Catalogue

Quality Criteria	✓	Which of the following quality criteria does the software tool enforce?
PSN2QC1		Is the Required System Logical Data Model consistent with the Data Catalogue? (5)

Attribute Dependent Tests

Mandatory Relationships   None

Optional Relationships   None

Object Representation   None

Quality Criteria   None

PSN3 Logical System Specification

Each **Logical System Specification** has significance as the Module Product from the Logical System Specification Module. It consists of the Selected Technical System Option, the Technical Environment Description and the Logical Design. (4,5)

Mandatory Relationships	✓	Does the software tool ensure that each **Logical System Specification**
PSN3MR1		contains one and only one **Logical Design**? (5)
PSN3MR2		contains one and only one **Selected Technical System Option**? (4)
PSN3MR3		contains one and only one **Technical Environment Description**? (4)

Optional Relationships None

Attributes	✓	Which of the following attributes for each **Logical System Specification** does the software tool support?		
		Name	Description	Validation
PSN3A1		Identifier	ID of specification	Unique

Object Representation	✓	Does the software tool ensure that each **Logical System Specification** has the following object representation?

PSN3OB1		A **Logical System Specification** consists of
		    Logical Design
		    Selected Technical System Option
		    Technical Environment Description

Quality Criteria None

Chapter 12
Processing Specification

Attribute Dependent Tests

Mandatory Relationships   None

Optional Relationships   None

Object Representation   None

Quality Criteria   None

PSN4   Physical System Specification

Each **Physical System Specification** has significance as packaging together the Physical Design, Application Development Standards and the Physical Environment Specification. (6)

Mandatory Relationships	✓	Does the software tool ensure that each **Physical System Specification**
PSN4MR1		contains one and only one **Application Development Standards**? (6)
PSN4MR2		contains one and only one **Physical Design**? (6)
PSN4MR3		contains one and only one **Physical Environment Specification**? (6)

Optional Relationships   None

Attributes	✓	Which of the following attributes for each **Physical System Specification** does the software tool support?		
		Name	Description	Validation
PSN4A1		Identifier	ID of specification	Unique

Object Representation	✓	Does the software tool ensure that each **Physical System Specification** has the following object representation?
PSN4OB1		A **Physical System Specification** consists of **Application Development Standard** **Physical Design** **Physical Environment Specification**

Quality Criteria   None

Attribute Dependent Tests

Mandatory Relationships   None

Optional Relationships   None

Object Representation   None

Quality Criteria   None

13 Relational Data Analysis

This chapter contains tests for the following products and concepts:

Products

	RDA1	RDA Working Paper	254

Concepts

	RDA51	Relation	255
	RDA52	Candidate Key	256
	RDA53	not used	
	RDA54	Simple Key	258
	RDA55	Compound Key	259
	RDA56	Composite Key	260
	RDA57	Foreign Key	261

Testing Criteria for the SSADM
Version 4 Tools Conformance Scheme

RDA1 RDA Working Paper

Each **RDA Working Paper** has significance as documenting the progress through relational data analysis, taking relations which are un-normalised through to third normal form. (3)

Mandatory Relationships   None

Optional Relationships   None

Attributes

✓	Which of the following attributes for each **RDA Working Paper** does the software tool support?		
	Name	Description	Validation
RDA1A1	Identifier	ID of working paper	Unique
RDA1A2	Name	Description	Validation

Object Representation   None

Quality Criteria   None

Attribute Dependent Tests

Mandatory Relationships   None

Optional Relationships   None

Object Representation   None

Quality Criteria   None

RDA51 Relation

Each **Relation** has significance as a group of data items (or attributes). (3)

Mandatory Relationships	✓	Does the software tool ensure that each **Relation**	
RDA51MR1		is consistent with one or more **Attribute Type**? (3)	
RDA51MR2		contains one or more **Candidate Key**? (3)	

Optional Relationships	✓	Does the software tool allow a **Relation**	
RDA51OR1		to contain one or more **Foreign Key**? (3)	

Attributes		✓	Which of the following attributes for each **Relation** does the software tool support?		
			Name	Description	Validation
RDA51A1			Name	Name of Relation	Unique ID
RDA51A2			Type	Type of Relation	UNF/INF/2NF/ 3NF/OPTIMISED

Object Representation   None

Quality Criteria	✓	Which of the following quality criteria does the software tool enforce?
RDA51QC1		Is each data item/attribute name unique? (3)

Attribute Dependent Tests

Mandatory Relationships   None

Testing Criteria for the SSADM
Version 4 Tools Conformance Scheme

Where Attribute: Type = 'OPTIMISED'

Optional Relationships	✓	Does the software tool allow a **Relation**
RDA51ADOR1		to represent one and only one **Entity Type**? (3)

Object Representation   None

Where Attribute: Type = 'OPTIMISED'

Quality Criteria	✓	Which of the following quality criteria does the software tool enforce?
RDA51ADQC1		Have all relations with the same primary key been merged into one relation? (3)

RDA52 Candidate Key

Each **Candidate Key** has significance as an attribute or set of attributes that uniquely identifies a relation. (3)

Mandatory Relationships	✓	Does the software tool ensure that each **Candidate Key**
RDA52MR1		identifies one and only one **Relation**? (3)
RDA52MR2		is one and only one **Simple Key**? (3) OR is one and only one **Compound Key**? (3) OR is one and only one **Composite Key**? (3)

Optional Relationships   None

Chapter 13
Relational Data Analysis

Attributes	✓	Which of the following attributes for each **Candidate Key** does the software tool support?		
		Name	Description	Validation
RDA52A1		Name	Name of key	Unique ID
RDA52A2		Primary	Primary key flag	Boolean

Object Representation   None

Quality Criteria   None

Attribute Dependent Tests

Mandatory Relationships   None

Where attribute: Primary = "TRUE"

Optional Relationships	✓	Does the software tool allow a **Candidate Key**
RDA52ADOR1		to be one or more **Foreign Key**? (3)

Object Representation   None

Quality Criteria   None

257

RDA54 Simple Key

Each **Simple Key** has significance as a candidate key which consists of one or more attributes. (3)

Mandatory Relationships	✓	Does the software tool ensure that each **Simple Key**	
RDA54MR1		is one and only one **Candidate Key**? (3)	
RDA54MR2		consists of one or more **Attribute Type**? (3)	

Optional Relationships None

Attributes	✓	Which of the following attributes for each **Simple Key** does the software tool support?		
		Name	Description	Validation
RDA54A1		Name	Name of key	Existing candidate key

Object Representation None

Quality Criteria None

Attribute Dependent Tests

Mandatory Relationships None

Optional Relationships None

Object Representation None

Quality Criteria None

RDA55 Compound Key

Each **Compound Key** has significance as a candidate key which consist of two or more foreign keys. (3)

Mandatory Relationships	✓	Does the software tool ensure that each **Compound Key**	
RDA55MR1		is one and only one **Candidate Key**? (3)	
RDA55MR2		consists of *two* or more **Foreign Key**? (3)	

Optional Relationships   None

Attributes	✓	Which of the following attributes for each **Compound Key** does the software tool support?		
		Name	**Description**	**Validation**
RDA55A1		Name	Name of key	Existing candidate key

Object Representation   None

Quality Criteria   None

Attribute Dependent Tests

Mandatory Relationships   None

Optional Relationships   None

Object Representation   None

Quality Criteria   None

RDA56 Composite Key

Each **Composite Key** has significance as a candidate key which contains a foreign key and a non-key. (3)

Mandatory Relationships	✓	Does the software tool ensure that each **Composite Key**
RDA56MR1		is one and only one **Candidate Key**? (3)
RDA56MR2		consists of one or more **Attribute Type**? (3)
RDA56MR3		consists of one or more **Foreign Key**? (3)

Optional Relationships   None

Attributes	✓	Which of the following attributes for each **Composite Key** does the software tool support?		
		Name	Description	Validation
RDA56A1		Name	Name of key	Existing candidate key

Object Representation   None

Quality Criteria   None

Attribute Dependent Tests

Mandatory Relationships   None

Optional Relationships   None

Object Representation   None

Quality Criteria   None

Chapter 13
Relational Data Analysis

RDA57 Foreign Key

Each Foreign Key has significance as an attribute or group of attributes in one relation that corresponds to a candidate key in another (or the same) relation.(3)

Mandatory Relationships	✓	Does the software tool ensure that each **Foreign Key**	
RDA57MR1		is part of one and only one **Relation**? (3)	
RDA57MR2		corresponds to one and only one **Candidate Key**? (3)	

Optional Relationships	✓	Does the software tool allow a **Foreign Key**	
RDA57OR1		to be part of one or more **Compound Key**? (3)	
RDA57OR2		to be part of one or more **Composite Key**? (3)	

Attributes	✓	Which of the following attributes for each **Foreign Key** does the software tool support?		
		Name	Description	Validation
RDA57A1		Name	Name of key	Existing candidate key

Object Representation   None

Quality Criteria   None

261

Attribute Dependent Tests

Mandatory Relationships None

Optional Relationships None

Object Representation None

Quality Criteria None

Chapter 14
Requirements Definition

14 Requirements Definition

This chapter contains tests for the following products and concepts:

Products

RDF1	Requirements Catalogue	264
RDF2	Take-On Requirements Description	265
RDF3	Training Requirements Description	266
RDF4	User Catalogue	267
RDF5	not used	
RDF6	User Manual Requirements Description	268
RDF7	Current Services Description	269
RDF8	Requirements Specification	271

Concepts

RDF51	Functional Requirement	272
RDF52	Non-Functional Requirement	274
RDF53	Service Level Requirement	276
RDF54	User Catalogue Entry	277

Testing Criteria for the SSADM
Version 4 Tools Conformance Scheme

RDF1 Requirements Catalogue

Each **Requirements Catalogue** has significance as the central repository for information covering all identified requirements, both functional and non-functional. (0,1,3,5) (2,6)

Mandatory Relationships	✓	Does the software tool ensure that each **Requirements Catalogue**
RDF1MR1		belongs to one and only one **Physical Process Specification**? (6)
RDF1MR2		belongs to one and only one **Requirements Specification**? (3)
RDF1MR3		contains one or more **Functional Requirement**? (0,1,3,5)
RDF1MR4		belongs to one and only one **Logical Design**? (5)

Optional Relationships   None

Attributes	✓	Which of the following attributes for each **Requirements Catalogue** does the software tool support?		
		Name	Description	Validation
RDF1A1		Name	Name of Catalogue	Unique Identifier

Object Representation	✓	Does the software tool ensure that each **Requirements Catalogue** has the following object representation?
RDF1OB1		A **Requirements Catalogue** consists of a set of **Functional Requirement**

Quality Criteria   None

264

Chapter 14
Requirements Definition

Attribute Dependent Tests

Mandatory Relationships None

Optional Relationships None

Object Representation None

Quality Criteria None

RDF2 Take-On Requirements Description

Each **Take-On Requirements Description** has significance as detailing the data conversion requirements which are to be implemented before a fully working system can be available. (4)

Mandatory Relationships None

Optional Relationships	✓	Does the software tool allow a **Take-On Requirements Description**		
RDF2OR1		to support one and only one **Impact Analysis**? (4)		

Attributes	✓	Which of the following attributes for each **Take-On Requirements Description** does the software tool support?		
		Name	Description	Validation
RDF2A1		Identifier	ID of Description	Unique Identifier
RDF2A2		Description	Description details	Text

Object Representation None

Quality Criteria None

265

Testing Criteria for the SSADM
Version 4 Tools Conformance Scheme

Attribute Dependent Tests

Mandatory Relationships None

Optional Relationships None

Object Representation None

Quality Criteria None

RDF3   Training Requirements Description

Each **Training Requirements Description** has significance as documenting the amount of training required for staff who will be using / working on the new system, so that they will be fully effective at the appropriate time (that is when the system is available for use). (4)

Mandatory Relationships None

Optional Relationships	✓	Does the software tool allow a **Training Requirements Description**
RDF3OR1		to support one and only one **Impact Analysis**? (4)

Attributes	✓	Which of the following attributes for each **Training Requirements Description** does the software tool support?		
		Name	Description	Validation
RDF3A1		Identifier	ID of Description	Unique Identifier
RDF3A2		Description	Description details	Text

Object Representation None

Quality Criteria None

Chapter 14
Requirements Definition

Attribute Dependent Tests

Mandatory Relationships None

Optional Relationships None

Object Representation None

Quality Criteria None

RDF4 User Catalogue

Each **User Catalogue** has significance as providing a description of the on-line users of the proposed system. (0,1) (2,3)

Mandatory Relationships	✓	Does the software tool ensure that each **User Catalogue**
RDF4MR1		contains one or more **User Catalogue Entry**? (0,1)

Optional Relationships None

Attributes	✓	Which of the following attributes for each **User Catalogue** does the software tool support?		
		Name	Description	Validation
RDF4A1		Name	Name of Catalogue	Unique Identifier

Object Representation None

Quality Criteria None

267

Testing Criteria for the SSADM
Version 4 Tools Conformance Scheme

Attribute Dependent Tests

Mandatory Relationships   None

Optional Relationships   None

Object Representation   None

Quality Criteria   None

RDF6   User Manual Requirements Description

Each **User Manual Requirements Description** has significance as documenting the basic information which can be supplied from the SSADM products and other available sources. It relates to the system and its smooth running from the user's point of view. (4)

Mandatory Relationships   None

Optional Relationships	✓	Does the software tool allow a **User Manual Requirements Description**		
RDF6OR1		to support one and only one **Impact Analysis**? (4)		

Attributes	✓	Which of the following attributes for each **User Manual Requirements Description** does the software tool support?		
		Name	Description	Validation
RDF6A1		Identifier	ID of Description	Unique Identifier
RDF6A2		Description	Description details	Text

Object Representation   None

Quality Criteria   None

268

Chapter 14
Requirements Definition

Attribute Dependent Tests

Mandatory Relationships None

Optional Relationships None

Object Representation None

Quality Criteria None

RDF7 Current Services Description

Each **Current Services Description** has significance as providing the details of the logicalised current system which, with the Requirements Catalogue and User Catalogue, is output from Stage 1: Investigation of Current Environment. (1) (2)

Mandatory Relationships	✓	Does the software tool ensure that each **Current Services Description**
RDF7MR1		contains one and only one **Data Catalogue**? (1)
RDF7MR2		contains one and only one **Logical Data Model**? (1)
RDF7MR3		contains one and only one **Context Diagram**? (1)
RDF7MR4		contains one and only one **Data Flow Model**? (1)
RDF7MR5		contains one and only one **Logical Data Store/ Entity Cross-Reference**? (1)

Optional Relationships None

Testing Criteria for the SSADM
Version 4 Tools Conformance Scheme

Attributes	✓	Which of the following attributes for each **Current Services Description** does the software tool support?		
		Name	**Description**	**Validation**
RDF7A1		Identifier	ID of CSD	Unique

Object Representation	✓	Does the software tool ensure that each **Current Services Description** has the following object representation?

RDF7OB1		A **Current Services Description** consists of
		    Data Catalogue
		    Logical Data Model
		    Context Diagram
		    Data Flow Model
		    Logical Data Store/Entity Cross-Reference

Quality Criteria	✓	Which of the following quality criteria does the software tool enforce?
RDF7QC1		Are the Context Diagram and the Logical Flow Model mutually consistent? (1)
RDF7QC2		Is the Current Environment Logical Data Model consistent with the Data Catalogue? (1)
RDF7QC3		Are the main elementary data stores on the DFM mapped on the Logical Data Store/Entity Cross-reference? (1)
RDF7QC4		Where logically related grouping of entities are shown on the Logical Data Store/Entity Cross-reference, is the structure consistent with the Logical Data Structure? (1)
RDF7QC5		Are any transient data stores represented on the Logical Data Store/Entity Cross-reference? (1)

Attribute Dependent Tests

Mandatory Relationships   None

Optional Relationships   None

Chapter 14
Requirements Definition

Object Representation   None

Quality Criteria   None

RDF8   Requirements Specification

Each **Requirements Specification** has significance as the module product from the Requirements Specification Module, packaging all of the details which are required in order to decide upon the technical direction of the project. (3)

Mandatory Relationships	✓	Does the software tool ensure that each **Requirements Specification**
RDF8MR1		contains one and only one **Data Catalogue**? (3)
RDF8MR2		contains one and only one **Processing Specification**? (3)
RDF8MR3		contains one and only one **Requirements Catalogue**? (3)

Optional Relationships   None

Attributes	✓	Which of the following attributes for each **Requirements Specification** does the software tool support?		
		Name	Description	Validation
RDF8A1		Identifier	ID of requirements specification	Unique

Object Representation	✓	Does the software tool ensure that each **Requirements Specification** has the following object representation?

RDF8OB1		A **Requirements Specification** consists of
		    Data Catalogue
		    Processing Specification
		    Requirements Catalogue

Testing Criteria for the SSADM
Version 4 Tools Conformance Scheme

Quality Criteria	✓	Which of the following quality criteria does the software tool enforce?
RDF8QC1		Is the Data Catalogue consistent with the Required System Logical Data Model? (3)
RDF8QC2		Is the Requirements Catalogue cross-referenced to the Function Definitions? (3)

Attribute Dependent Tests

Mandatory Relationships   None

Optional Relationships   None

Object Representation   None

Quality Criteria   None

RDF51 Functional Requirement

Each **Functional Requirement** has significance as a description of a required feature of a proposed new system. (0,1,3,5)

Mandatory Relationships	✓	Does the software tool ensure that each **Functional Requirement**
RDF51MR1		belongs to one and only one **Requirements Catalogue**? (0,1,3,5)
RDF51MR2		gives rise to one and only one **Function Definition**? (3)

Chapter 14
Requirements Definition

Optional Relationships	✓	Does the software tool allow a **Functional Requirement**		
RDF51OR1		to reference one or more **Non-Functional Requirement**? (0,1,3,5)		
RDF51OR2		to reference one or more **Functional Requirement**? (0,1,3,5)		
RDF51OR3		to be referenced by one or more **Functional Requirement**? (0,1,3,5)		
Attributes	✓	Which of the following attributes for each **Functional Requirement** does the software tool support?		
		Name	Description	Validation
RDF51A1		Identifier	ID of requirement	Unique ID
RDF51A2		Source	Source of requirement	Text
RDF51A3		Priority	Priority of requirement	Text
RDF51A4		Owner	Owner of requirement	Text
RDF51A5		Description	Description of requirement	Text
RDF51A6		Benefits	Benefits of requirement	Text
RDF51A7		Comments	Suggested Solution	Text
RDF51A8		Related documents	Reference to any related documentation	Text
RDF51A9		Related requirements	Reference to any related requirements	Text
RDF51A10		Resolution	Note on how requirement is achieved	Text

273

Testing Criteria for the SSADM
Version 4 Tools Conformance Scheme

Object Representation   None

Quality Criteria	✓	Which of the following quality criteria does the software tool enforce?
RDF51QC1		Have the source, owner, priority and benefit been identified? (0,1,3,5)

Attribute Dependent Tests

Mandatory Relationships   None

Optional Relationships   None

Object Representation   None

Quality Criteria   None

RDF52 Non-Functional Requirement

Each **Non-Functional Requirement** has significance as a description of how a required feature should be provided, or how well or to what level of quality, performance or reliability. (0,1,3,5)

Mandatory Relationships	✓	Does the software tool ensure that each **Non-Functional Requirement**
RDF52MR1		further describes one and only one **Functional Requirement**? (0,1,3,5)

Optional Relationships	✓	Does the software tool allow a **Non-Functional Requirement**
RDF52OR1		to reference one or more **Service Level Requirement**? (0,1,3,5)

Chapter 14
Requirements Definition

Attributes	✓	Which of the following attributes for each **Non-Functional Requirement** does the software tool support?		
		Name	Description	Validation
RDF52A1		Identifier	ID of requirement	Unique ID
RDF52A2		Description	Description of requirement	Text
RDF52A3		Target value	Desired value of requirement	Text
RDF52A4		Acceptable	Range of Acceptance	Text
RDF52A5		Comments	Note	Text

Object Representation   None

Quality Criteria   None

Attribute Dependent Tests

Mandatory Relationships   None

Optional Relationships   None

Object Representation   None

Quality Criteria   None

275

Testing Criteria for the SSADM
Version 4 Tools Conformance Scheme

RDF53 Service Level Requirement

Each **Service Level Requirement** has significance as a non-functional requirement that states the required quality of service that a user expects from a functional aspect of a system. (0,1,3,5)

Mandatory Relationships	✓	Does the software tool ensure that each **Service Level Requirement**
RDF53MR1		further describes one and only one **Non-Functional Requirement**? (0,1,3,5)
RDF53MR2		further describes one and only one **Function Definition**? (3)

Optional Relationships   None

Attributes		✓	Which of the following attributes for each **Service Level Requirement** does the software tool support?	
			Name	Description	Validation
RDF53A1		Identifier	ID of requirement	Unique ID
RDF53A2		SL Description	Description of requirement	Text
RDF53A3		SL Target Value	Desired value of requirement	Text
RDF53A4		SL Range	Range of Acceptance	Text
RDF53A5		SL Comments	Note	Text

Object Representation   None

Quality Criteria   None

Chapter 14
Requirements Definition

Attribute Dependent Tests

Mandatory Relationships   None

Optional Relationships   None

Object Representation   None

Quality Criteria   None

RDF54 User Catalogue Entry

Each **User Catalogue Entry** has significance as providing details of job titles and the tasks undertaken by each of the identified users. (0,1) (2,3)

Mandatory Relationships	✓	Does the software tool ensure that each **User Catalogue Entry**		
RDF54MR1		belongs to one and only one **User Catalogue**? (0,1)		

Optional Relationships	✓	Does the software tool allow a **User Catalogue Entry**		
RDF54OR1		to detail one and only one **User Role**? (3)		

Attributes	✓	Which of the following attributes for each **User Catalogue Entry** does the software tool support?		
		Name	Description	Validation
RDF54A1		Identifier	ID of job	Unique
RDF54A2		Job Title	User's job title	Text
RDF54A3		Activities	All the job activities performed by the user	Text

Object Representation   None

277

Quality Criteria   None

Attribute Dependent Tests

Mandatory Relationships   None

Optional Relationships   None

Object Representation   None

Quality Criteria   None

15 Specification Prototyping

This chapter contains tests for the following products and concepts:

Products	SPP1	Prototype Demonstration Objective Document	280
	SPP2	Prototype Pathway	281
	SPP3	Prototype Result Log	283
	SPP4	Prototyping Report	284
Concepts	SPP51	Prototype Pathway Component	285
	SPP52	Prototype Pathway Component Query	287
	SPP53	Prototype Pathway Component Result	289

SPP1 Prototype Demonstration Objective Document

Each **Prototype Demonstration Objective Document** has significance as a document completed prior to any prototype demonstration for each Prototype Pathway. Assumptions and queries for each menu, screen and / or report are listed under their respective component number. This document lists the points of discussion to be addressed between the user and the analyst during the prototype demonstration. (3)

Mandatory Relationships	✓	Does the software tool ensure that each **Prototype Demonstration Objective Document**
SPP1MR1		is for one and only one **Prototype Pathway**? (3)
SPP1MR2		contains one or more **Prototype Pathway Component Query**? (3)

Optional Relationships   None

Attributes	✓	Which of the following attributes for each **Prototype Demonstration Objective Document** does the software tool support?		
		Name	Description	Validation
SPP1A1		Identifier	Document number	Unique for pathway
SPP1A2		Pathway No.	Prototype pathway number	Existing prototype pathway
SPP1A3		Function name	Name of function being prototyped	Existing function
SPP1A4		User role	User role performing the function	Existing user role
SPP1A5		Agenda	Agenda of the prototyping	Text

Object Representation   None

Chapter 15
Specification Prototyping

Quality Criteria   None

Attribute Dependent Tests

Object Representation   None

Quality Criteria   None

SPP2   Prototype Pathway

Each **Prototype Pathway** has significance as combining screen and report components with existing menus. The pathways are a script for the prototyping session and hence use a limited and simple serial diagrammatic representation.(3)

Mandatory Relationships	✓	Does the software tool ensure that each **Prototype Pathway**
SPP2MR1		is for one and only one **User Role**? (3)
SPP2MR2		is for one and only one **Function**? (3)
SPP2MR3		is documented by one or more **Prototype Demonstration Objective Document**? (3)
SPP2MR4		is documented by one or more **Prototype Result Log**? (3)
SPP2MR5		contains one or more **Prototype Pathway Component**? (3)

Optional Relationships   None

281

Testing Criteria for the SSADM
Version 4 Tools Conformance Scheme

Attributes	✓	Which of the following attributes for each **Prototype Pathway** does the software tool support?		
		Name	Description	Validation
SPP2A1		Identifier	Document number	Unique for pathway
SPP2A2		Function name	Name of function being prototyped	Existing function
SPP2A3		User role	User role performing the function	Existing user role
SPP2A4		Pathway No.	Prototype pathway number	Existing prototype pathway

Object Representation	✓	Does the software tool ensure that each **Prototype Pathway** has the following object representation?
SPP2OB1		A **Prototype Pathway** consists of **Prototype Pathway Component**

Quality Criteria	✓	Which of the following quality criteria does the software tool enforce?
SPP2QC1		Does the Prototype Pathway represent one dialogue or report or both for one user role? (3)

Attribute Dependent Tests

Object Representation   None

Quality Criteria   None

Chapter 15
Specification Prototyping

SPP3 Prototype Result Log

Each **Prototype Result Log** has significance as recording the results of the prototype demonstration. This document is used in a similar capacity to minutes of a meeting. Each request made by the user is documented on the log, with a change grade, and the log is updated later to show what changes are required. (3)

Mandatory Relationships	✓	Does the software tool ensure that each **Prototype Result Log**
SPP3MR1		is for one and only one **Prototype Pathway**? (3)
SPP3MR2		contains one or more **Prototype Pathway Component Result**? (3)

Optional Relationships   None

Attributes		✓	Which of the following attributes for each **Prototype Result Log** does the software tool support?		
			Name	Description	Validation
SPP3A1			Identifier	Log number	Unique for pathway
SPP3A2			Pathway No.	Prototype pathway number	Existing prototype pathway
SPP3A3			Function name	Name of function being prototyped	Existing function‡
SPP3A4			User role	User role performing the function	Existing user role‡

Object Representation   None

Quality Criteria   None

283

Testing Criteria for the SSADM
Version 4 Tools Conformance Scheme

Attribute Dependent Tests

Object Representation   None

Quality Criteria   None

SPP4 Prototyping Report

Each **Prototyping Report** has significance as documenting whether the objectives for the prototyping exercise were achieved, or alternatively, the reasons why they were not. It includes estimates of the value of the work done and where necessary suggests whether more work would (or would not) be beneficial. (3)

Mandatory Relationships   None

Optional Relationships   None

Attributes	✓	Which of the following attributes for each **Prototyping Report** does the software tool support?		
		Name	Description	Validation
SPP4A1		Identifier	Report ID	Unique
SPP4A2		Description	Content of report	Text

Object Representation   None

Quality Criteria   None

Attribute Dependent Tests

Object Representation   None

Quality Criteria   None

Chapter 15
Specification Prototyping

SPP51 Prototype Pathway Component

Each **Prototype Pathway Component** has significance as an identifiable component on a prototype pathway.(3)

Mandatory Relationships	✓	Does the software tool ensure that each **Prototype Pathway Component**
SPP51MR1		is part of one and only one **Prototype Pathway**? (3)

Optional Relationships	✓	Does the software tool allow a **Prototype Pathway Component**
SPP51OR1		to be questioned using one or more **Prototype Pathway Component Query**? (3)
SPP51OR2		to be answered by one or more **Prototype Pathway Component Result**? (3)

Attributes		✓	Which of the following attributes for each **Prototype Pathway Component** does the software tool support?		
			Name	Description	Validation
	SPP51A1		Identifier	Prototype pathway number	Existing prototype pathway
	SPP51A2		Comp. Type	Type of component	MENU/ DIALOGUE/ SCREEN/ REPORT
	SPP51A3		Comp. Type ID	ID of component type	Existing menu ID /dialogue ID /screen ID /report ID
	SPP51A4		Description	Description of component	Text
	SPP51A5		Component No.	Number of component	Integer

Object Representation   None

285

Testing Criteria for the SSADM
Version 4 Tools Conformance Scheme

Quality Criteria   None

Attribute Dependent Tests

Where Attribute: Type = "MENU"

Object Representation	✓	Does the software tool ensure that each **Prototype Pathway Component** has the following object representation for the given attribute value?
SPP51ADOB1		Menu id: <Menu id> <Menu name> <Component Number>

Where Attribute: Type = "DIALOGUE"

Object Representation	✓	Does the software tool ensure that each **Prototype Pathway Component** has the following object representation for the given attribute value?
SPP51ADOB2		Dialogue id: <Dialogue id> <Dialogue name> <Component Number>

Where Attribute: Type = "SCREEN"

Object Representation	✓	Does the software tool ensure that each **Prototype Pathway Component** has the following object representation for the given attribute value?
SPP51ADOB3		Screen LDGE: <LDGE id> <LDGE name> <Function name> <Component Number>

Chapter 15
Specification Prototyping

Where Attribute: Type = "REPORT"

Object Representation	✓	Does the software tool ensure that each **Prototype Pathway Component** has the following object representation for the given attribute value?
SPP51ADOB4		Report id: \<Report id\> \<Report name\> \<Function name\> \<Component Number\>

Quality Criteria   None

SPP52   Prototype Pathway Component Query

Each **Prototype Pathway Component Query** has significance as a question for a prototype pathway component. (3)

Mandatory Relationships	✓	Does the software tool ensure that each **Prototype Pathway Component Query**
SPP52MR1		is for one and only one **Prototype Pathway Component**? (3)
SPP52MR2		is documented in one and only one **Prototype Demonstration Objective Document**? (3)

Optional Relationships	✓	Does the software tool allow a **Prototype Pathway Component Query**
SPP52OR1		to be resolved by one or more **Prototype Pathway Component Result**? (3)

Testing Criteria for the SSADM
Version 4 Tools Conformance Scheme

Attributes	✓	Which of the following attributes for each **Prototype Pathway Component** does the software tool support?		
		Name	Description	Validation
SPP52A1		Identifier	Prototype pathway number	Existing prototype pathway
SPP52A2		Component No.	Number of component	Existing component
SPP52A3		Query No.	Number of query	Integer
SPP52A4		Query	Component Query	Text

Object Representation   None

Quality Criteria   None

Attribute Dependent Tests

Object Representation   None

Quality Criteria   None

Chapter 15
Specification Prototyping

SPP53 Prototype Pathway Component Result

Each **Prototype Pathway Component Result** has significance as a result for a prototype pathway component query. (3)

Mandatory Relationships	✓	Does the software tool ensure that each **Prototype Pathway Component Result**
SPP53MR1		is for one and only one **Prototype Pathway Component**? (3)
SPP53MR2		is documented in one and only one **Prototype Result Log**? (3)
SPP53MR3		is the resolution for one or more **Prototype Pathway Component Query**? (3)

Optional Relationships   None

Attributes	✓	Which of the following attributes for each **Prototype Pathway Component** does the software tool support?		
		Name	Description	Validation
SPP53A1		Identifier	Prototype pathway number	Existing prototype pathway
SPP53A2		Component No.	Number of component	Existing component
SPP53A3		Result No.	Number of result	Integer
SPP53A4		Description	Description of result	Text
SPP53A5		Grade	Grade of change	N/C/D/P/S/A/G

Object Representation   None

Testing Criteria for the SSADM
Version 4 Tools Conformance Scheme

Quality Criteria	✓	Which of the following quality criteria does the software tool enforce?
SPP53QC1		Has a change grade been allocated to each result?

Attribute Dependent Tests

Object Representation   None

Quality Criteria   None

16 Technical System Options

This chapter contains tests for the following products and concepts:

Products

TSO1	Capacity Planning Input	292
TSO2	System Description	293
TSO3	Technical Environment Description	294
TSO4	Technical System Options	295
TSO5	Selected Technical System Option	296

Concepts

TSO51	Technical System Option	297

TSO1 Capacity Planning Input

Each **Capacity Planning Input** has significance as passing processing and data information outside SSADM activities to capacity planning techniques, explicitly during development of Technical System Options. (4)

Mandatory Relationships	✓	Does the software tool ensure that each **Capacity Planning Input**
TSO1MR1		is produced for one and only one **Technical System Option**? (4) OR is produced for one and only one **Selected Technical System Option**? (4)

Optional Relationships None

Attributes		✓	Which of the following attributes for each **Capacity Planning Input** does the software tool support?		
			Name	Description	Validation
TSO1A1			Identifier	ID of input	Unique identifier
TSO1A2			Description	Description of input	Text

Object Representation None

Quality Criteria None

Attribute Dependent Tests

Object Representation None

Quality Criteria None

TSO2 System Description

Each **System Description** has significance as showing how the Requirements Specification is met by the Technical Environment Description for a particular Technical System Option. In many cases the major decisions in this area will already have been taken in choosing a Business System Option.(4)

Mandatory Relationships	✓	Does the software tool ensure that each **System Description**
TSO2MR1		is for one and only one **Technical Environment Description**? (4)

Optional Relationships   None

Attributes	✓	Which of the following attributes for each **System Description** does the software tool support?		
		Name	Description	Validation
TSO2A1 TSO2A2		Identifier Description	ID of description Description of description	Unique identifier Text

Object Representation   None

Quality Criteria   None

Attribute Dependent Tests

Object Representation   None

Quality Criteria   None

TSO3 Technical Environment Description

Each **Technical Environment Description** has significance as providing the specification of the technical environment which is produced once the Technical System Option has been selected. This detail is then passed on to physical design activities.(4)

Mandatory Relationships	✓	Does the software tool ensure that each **Technical Environment Description**
TSO3MR1		is shown by one and only one **System Description**? (4)
TSO3MR2		is for one and only one **Selected Technical System Option**? (4)
TSO3MR3		belongs to one and only one **Logical System Specification**? (4)

Optional Relationships	✓	Does the software tool allow a **Technical Environment Description**
TSO3OR1		to be documented by one and only one **Impact Analysis**? (4)

Attributes		✓	Which of the following attributes for each **Technical Environment Description** does the software tool support?		
			Name	Description	Validation
TSO3A1			Identifier	ID of TED	Unique identifier
TSO3A2			Description	Description of TED	Text

Object Representation   None

Quality Criteria   None

Attribute Dependent Tests

Object Representation None

Quality Criteria None

TSO4 Technical System Options

Each **Technical System Options** has significance as the set of Technical System Options which have been developed so that the system development direction can be chosen. (4)

Mandatory Relationships	✓	Does the software tool ensure that each **Technical System Options**
TSO4MR1		contains one or more **Technical System Option**? (4)

Optional Relationships None

Attributes	✓	Which of the following attributes for each **Technical System Options** does the software tool support?		
		Name	Description	Validation
TSO4A1		Identifier	ID of Set	Unique identifier

Object Representation None

Quality Criteria None

Attribute Dependent Tests

Object Representation None

Quality Criteria None

TSO5 Selected Technical System Option

Each **Selected Technical System Option** has significance as documenting the selection process with the planning details. The technical details are placed in the Technical Environment Description. (2, 4)

Mandatory Relationships	✓	Does the software tool ensure that each **Selected Technical System Option**
TSO5MR1		is based on one or more **Technical System Option**? (4)
TSO5MR2		belongs to one and only one **Logical System Specification**? (4)

Optional Relationships	✓	Does the software tool allow a **Selected Technical System Option**
TSO5OR1		to be further specified by one and only one **Technical Environment Description**? (4)
TSO5OR2		to be documented by one and only one **Cost/Benefit Analysis**? (4)
TSO5OR3		to be documented by one and only one **Impact Analysis**? (4)
TSO5OR4		to be the basis for one and only one **Capacity Planning Input**? (4)

Attributes		✓	Which of the following attributes for each **Selected Technical System Option** does the software tool support?	
		Name	Description	Validation
TSO5A1		Identifier	ID of selected option	Unique identifier
TSO5A2		Description	Description of selected option	Text

Object Representation   None

Quality Criteria   None

Attribute Dependent Tests

Mandatory Relationships   None

Optional Relationships   None

Object Representation   None

Quality Criteria   None

TSO51 Technical System Option

Each **Technical System Option** has significance as providing the detailed implementation plan for the Selected Business System Option. (4)

Mandatory Relationships	✓	Does the software tool ensure that each **Technical System Option**
TSO51MR1		belongs to one and only one **Technical System Option**? (4)
TSO51MR2		is based on one and only one **Selected Business System Option**? (4)

Testing Criteria for the SSADM
Version 4 Tools Conformance Scheme

Optional Relationships	✓	Does the software tool allow a **Technical System Option**		
TSO51OR1		to be the basis for one and only one **Selected Technical System Option**? (4)		
TSO51OR2		to be documented by one and only one **Cost/Benefit Analysis**? (4)		
TSO51OR3		to be documented by one and only one **Impact Analysis**? (4)		
TSO51OR4		to be the basis for one and only one **Capacity Planning Input**? (4)		

Attributes	✓	Which of the following attributes for each **Technical System Option** does the software tool support?		
		Name	Description	Validation
TSO51A1		Identifier	Name/Number of option	Unique identifier
TSO51A2		Description	Description of option	Text

Object Representation   None

Quality Criteria   None

Attribute Dependent Tests

Object Representation   None

Quality Criteria   None

17 Physical Data Design

This chapter contains tests for the following products:

Products

	PDD1	Physical Data Design	300
	PDD2	Physical Design Strategy	301
	PDD3	Physical Design	302

PDD1 Physical Data Design

Each **Physical Data Design** has significance as the definition for the physical database which is to be implemented. (6)

Mandatory Relationships	✓	Does the software tool ensure that each **Physical Data Design**
PDD1MR1		belongs to one and only one **Physical Design**? (6)

Optional Relationships   None

Attributes		✓	Which of the following attributes for each **Physical Data Design** does the software tool support?		
			Name	Description	Validation
PDD1A1			Identifier	ID of physical data design	Unique
PDD1A2			Description	Description of database design	Text

Object Representation   None

Quality Criteria   None

Attribute Dependent Tests

Object Representation   None

Quality Criteria   None

Chapter 17
Physical Data Design

PDD2 Physical Design Strategy

Each **Physical Design Strategy** has significance as documenting all aspects relating to designing the physical implementation of the application. This includes all planning documentation. (6)

Mandatory Relationships	✓	Does the software tool ensure that each **Physical Design Strategy**
PDD2MR1		belongs to one and only one **Application Development Standards**? (6)

Optional Relationships   None

Attributes	✓	Which of the following attributes for each **Physical Design Strategy** does the software tool support?		
		Name	Description	Validation
PDD2A1		Identifier	ID of strategy	Unique
PDD2A2		Description	Description of Strategy	Text

Object Representation   None

Quality Criteria   None

Attribute Dependent Tests

Object Representation   None

Quality Criteria   None

PDD3 Physical Design

Each **Physical Design** has significance as the module product from the SSADM Physical Design Module and defines the data and processing elements of the implementable system (6)

Mandatory Relationships	✓	Does the software tool ensure that each **Physical Design**
PDD3MR1		contains one and only one **Physical Data Design**? (6)
PDD3MR2		contains one and only one **Physical Process Specification**? (6)
PDD3MR3		contains one and only one **Process Data Interface**? (6)
PDD3MR4		belongs to one and only one **Physical System Specification**? (6)

Optional Relationships   None

Attributes	✓	Which of the following attributes for each **Physical Design** does the software tool support?		
		Name	Description	Validation
PDD3A1		Identifier	ID of design	Unique

Object Representation	✓	Does the software tool ensure that each **Physical Design** has the following object representation?
PDD3OB1		A **Physical Design** consists of **Physical Data Design** **Physical Process Specification** **Process Data Interface**

Quality Criteria   None

Chapter 17
Physical Data Design

Attribute Dependent Tests

Mandatory Relationships None

Optional Relationships None

Object Representation None

Quality Criteria None

18 Physical Process Specification

This chapter contains tests for the following products and concepts:

Products

	PPS1	Function Component Implementation Map	306
	PPS2	Process Data Interface	307
	PPS3	Physical Process Specification	308

Testing Criteria for the SSADM
Version 4 Tools Conformance Scheme

PPS1 Function Component Implementation Map

Each **Function Component Implementation Map** has significance as a classification and specification of all implementation fragments for all function components defined in the Function Definitions to meet the processing requirements. (6)

Mandatory Relationships

	✓	Does the software tool ensure that each **Function Component Implementation Map**
PPS1MR1		belongs to one and only one **Physical Process Specification**? (6)

Optional Relationships None

Attributes

	✓	Which of the following attributes for each **Function Component Implementation Map** does the software tool support?		
		Name	Description	Validation
PPS1A1		Identifier	ID of FCIM	Unique
PPS1A2		Description	Description of processing specifications	text

Object Representation None

Quality Criteria

	✓	Which of the following quality criteria does the software tool enforce?
PPS1QC1		Is every function definition component implementation shown on the map? (6)
PPS1QC2		Is every function component cross-referenced to a fragment? (6)

Chapter 18
Physical Process Specification

Attribute Dependent Tests

Object Representation   None

Quality Criteria   None

PPS2   Process Data Interface

Each **Process Data Interface** has significance as documenting how the Logical Data Model can be mapped onto the Physical Data Design, showing how it interfaces with the Physical Processing Specification. (6)

Mandatory Relationships	✓	Does the software tool ensure that each **Process Data Interface**
PPS2MR1		belongs to one and only one **Physical Design**? (6)

Optional Relationships   None

Attributes	✓	Which of the following attributes for each **Process Data Interface** does the software tool support?		
		Name	Description	Validation
PPS2A1 PPS2A2		Identifier Description	ID of interface Description of interface	Unique text

Object Representation   None

Quality Criteria   None

307

Testing Criteria for the SSADM
Version 4 Tools Conformance Scheme

Attribute Dependent Tests

Object Representation   None

Quality Criteria   None

PPS3   Physical Process Specification

Each **Physical Process Specification** has significance as packaging all of the specifications for processing which are required in the proposed system. (6)

Mandatory Relationships	✓	Does the software tool ensure that each **Physical Process Specification**
PPS3MR1		belongs to one and only one **Physical Design**? (6)
PPS3MR2		contains one and only one **Function Component Implementation Map**? (6)
PPS3MR3		contains one and only one **Logical Data Model**? (6)
PPS3MR4		contains one and only one **Data Catalogue**? (6)
PPS3MR5		contains one and only one **Function Definitions**? (6)
PPS3MR6		contains one and only one **Requirements Catalogue**? (6)

Optional Relationships   None

Attributes	✓	Which of the following attributes for each **Physical Process Specification** does the software tool support?		
		Name	Description	Validation
PPS3A1		Identifier	ID of Specification	Unique

Chapter 18
Physical Process Specification

Object Representation	✓	Does the software tool ensure that each **Physical Process Specification** has the following object representation?

PPS3OB1		A **Physical Process Specification** consists of
		    Function Component Implementation Map
		    Logical Data Model
		    Data Catalogue
		    Function Definitions
		    Requirements Catalogue

Quality Criteria   None

Attribute Dependent Tests

Object Representation   None

Quality Criteria   None

19 Physical Environment Description

This chapter contains tests for the following products and concepts:

Products

	PED1	DBMS Data Storage Classification	312
	PED2	DBMS Performance Classification	314
	PED3	Physical Environment Classification	316
	PED4	not used	
	PED5	Processing System Classification	317

Testing Criteria for the SSADM
Version 4 Tools Conformance Scheme

PED1 DBMS Data Storage Classification

Each **DBMS Data Storage Classification** has significance as analysing and recording data storage and retrieval mechanisms of DBMS or file handler. (6)

Mandatory Relationships	✓	Does the software tool ensure that each **DBMS Data Storage Classification**
PED1MR1		belongs to one and only one **Physical Environment Classification**? (6)
PED1MR2		documents one or more **Relationship Representation**? (6)
PED1MR3		documents one and only one **Logical Key Representation**? (6)
PED1MR4		documents one or more **Mechanism For Retrieval By Key**? (6)
PED1MR5		documents one and only one **Implementation Of Place Near Logic**? (6)

Optional Relationships   None

Attributes		✓	Which of the following attributes for each **DBMS Data Storage Classification** does the software tool support?		
			Name	Description	Validation
PED1A1			Name	Name of handler	Unique
PED1A2			Relationship representation		
			Table	Table representation	Text
			List	List representation	Text
			Phantom	Phantom representation	Text

312

Chapter 19
Physical Environment Description

Attributes	✓	Which of the following attributes for each **DBMS Data Storage Classification** does the software tool support?		
		Name	Description	Validation
PED1A3		Amalgamation of entity and relationship data		
		None	None	Text
		Master	Relationship and master	Text
		Detail	Relationship and detail	Text
		Both	Relationship with master and detail	Text
		Relationship	Relationship and relationship	Text
PED1A4		Key Representation in relationship		
		From master	Master to detail /detail to next detail	Text
		From detail	Detail to master	Text
PED1A5		Retrieval by logical key		
		Search	Searching Mechanism	Text
		Indexing	Indexing Mechanism	Text
		Hashing	Hashing Mechanism	Text
PED1A6		Place Near	Implementation of Place Near Logic	Text
PED1A7		Restrictions	Notes on Significant restrictions	Text

313

Testing Criteria for the SSADM
Version 4 Tools Conformance Scheme

Object Representation   None

Quality Criteria   None

Attribute Dependent Tests

Object Representation   None

Quality Criteria   None

PED2   DBMS Performance Classification

Each **DBMS Performance Classification** has significance as recording the factors which impact on the performance of a DBMS or file handler. (6)

Mandatory Relationships	✓	Does the software tool ensure that each **DBMS Performance Classification**
PED2MR1		belongs to one and only one **Physical Environment Classification**? (6)

Optional Relationships   None

Attributes	✓	Which of the following attributes for each **DBMS Performance Classification** does the software tool support?		
		Name	Description	Validation
PED2A1		Name	Name of file handler	Unique
PED2A2		Txn O'head	Transaction logging overhead	Text
PED2A3		Recovery O'head	Recovery logging overhead	Text
PED2A4		Commit O'head	Commit/backout overhead	Text

314

Chapter 19
Physical Environment Description

Attributes	✓	Which of the following attributes for each **DBMS Performance Classification** does the software tool support?		
		Name	Description	Validation
PED2A5		Space O'head	Space management overhead	Text
PED2A6		Dialogue O'head	Dialogue context save/restore overhead	Text
PED2A7		Standard time factors		
		Read time	Time taken to read	Text
		Comment	Notes on reading	Text
		Write time	Time taken to write	Text
		Comment	Note on writing	Text
		Overflow	Notes on overflow overhead	Text
PED2A8		DBMS Operation		
		Operation	DBMS Operation	Text
		Processor	DBMS processor time	Text
		Monitor	TP monitor processor time	Text
PED2A9		Sort Packages	Performance parameters for available sort packages	Text

Object Representation   None

Quality Criteria   None

315

Testing Criteria for the SSADM
Version 4 Tools Conformance Scheme

Attribute Dependent Tests

Object Representation None

Quality Criteria None

PED3 Physical Environment Classification

Each **Physical Environment Classification** has significance as classifying the environment in which the application is to be implemented. Also describes the development environment and migration path where necessary. (6)

Mandatory Relationships	✓	Does the software tool ensure that each **Physical Environment Classification**
PED3MR1		belongs to one and only one **Application Development Standards**? (6)
PED3MR2		contains one and only one **DBMS Data Storage Classification**? (6)
PED3MR3		contains one and only one **DBMS Performance Classification**? (6)
PED3MR4		contains one and only one **Processing Systems Classification**? (6)

Optional Relationships None

Attributes	✓	Which of the following attributes for each **Physical Environment Classification** does the software tool support?		
		Name	Description	Validation
PED3A1		Identifier	ID of classification	Unique

Chapter 19
Physical Environment Description

Object Representation	✓	Does the software tool ensure that each **Physical Environment Classification** has the following object representation?
PED3OB1		A **Physical Environment Classification** consists of **DBMS Data Storage Classification** **DBMS Performance Classifiaction** **Processing System Classification**

Quality Criteria   None

Attribute Dependent Tests

Object Representation   None

Quality Criteria   None

PED5   Processing Systems Classification

Each **Processing Systems Classification** has significance as classifying the details of the processing environment which is to be used for implementation. Where appropriate, it also defines the development environment. (6)

Mandatory Relationships	✓	Does the software tool ensure that each **Processing Systems Classification**
PED5MR1		belongs to one and only one **Physical Environment Classification**? (6)

Optional Relationships   None

Testing Criteria for the SSADM
Version 4 Tools Conformance Scheme

Attributes	✓	Which of the following attributes for each **Processing Systems Classification** does the software tool support?		
		Name	Description	Validation
PED5A1		Identifier	Identifier of classification	Text
PED5A2		Tool feature	Classes of tool feature	Text
PED5A3		Procedural	Procedural/Non-procedural	Boolean
PED5A4		On-line	On-line/Off-line	'ON'/'OFF'
PED5A5		Success Units	Alternative commit strategies	Text
PED5A6		Errors	Error handling mechanisms	Text
PED5A7		Processing components	Description of processing combinations	Text
PED5A8		DB processing	Flexibility of db accessing	Text
PED5A9		Update	Update processes generated	Boolean
PED5A10		Enquiry	Enquiry processes generated	Boolean
PED5A11		I/O Processing	Grouping of data items	Text
PED5A12		Dialogue processing	Generating dialogue components	Text
PED5A13		Dialogue navigation	Mechanisms available for dialogue navigations	Text
PED5A14		PDI	Description of PDI	Text
PED5A15		Distributed systems	Description of distributed systems facilities	Text

Chapter 19
Physical Environment Description

Object Representation   None

Quality Criteria   None

Attribute Dependent Tests

Object Representation   None

Quality Criteria   None

Chapter 20
Miscellaneous

20 Miscellaneous

This chapter contains tests for the following products and concepts:

Products

	MIS1	Application Development Standards	322
	MIS2	Application Naming Standards	323
	MIS3	Application Style Guide	324
	MIS4	Installation Style Guide	325
	MIS5	Physical Environment Specification	327

Testing Criteria for the SSADM
Version 4 Tools Conformance Scheme

MIS1 Application Development Standards

Each **Application Development Standards** has significance as defining the standards which apply to the physical design and development activities, for this project / application. (4,6)

Mandatory Relationships	✓	Does the software tool ensure that each **Application Development Standards**
MIS1MR1		contains one and only one **Application Naming Standards**? (6)
MIS1MR2		contains one and only one **Application Style Guide**? (4)
MIS1MR3		contains one and only one **Physical Design Strategy**? (6)
MIS1MR4		contains one and only one **Physical Environment Classification**? (6)
MIS1MR5		belongs to one and only one **Physical System Specification**? (6)

Optional Relationships   None

Attributes	✓	Which of the following attributes for each **Application Development Standards** does the software tool support?		
		Name	Description	Validation
MIS1A1		Identifier	ID of standards	Unique

Object Representation	✓	Does the software tool ensure that each **Application Development Standards** has the following object representation?

MIS1OB1		An **Application Development Standards** consists of
		    Application Naming Standards
		    Application Style Guide
		    Physical Design Strategy
		    Physical Environment Classification

Chapter 20
Miscellaneous

Quality Criteria   None

Attribute Dependent Tests

Mandatory Relationships   None

Optional Relationships   None

Object Representation   None

Quality Criteria   None

MIS2   Application Naming Standards

Each **Application Naming Standards** has significance as defining the naming conventions for all aspects of the application under development, with particular emphasis being placed on constraints imposed by the (physical) implementation environment. (6)

Mandatory Relationships	✓	Does the software tool ensure that each **Application Naming Standards**
MIS2MR1		belongs to one and only one **Application Development Standards**? (6)

Optional Relationships   None

Attributes	✓	Which of the following attributes for each **Application Naming Standards** does the software tool support?		
		Name	Description	Validation
MIS2A1 MIS2A2		Identifier Description	ID of standards Description of standards	Unique Text

323

Testing Criteria for the SSADM
Version 4 Tools Conformance Scheme

Object Representation   None

Quality Criteria   None

Attribute Dependent Tests

Mandatory Relationships   None

Optional Relationships   None

Object Representation   None

Quality Criteria   None

MIS3 Application Style Guide

Each **Application Style Guide** has significance as a set of standards, covering the user interface, to be followed within a particular application development. This document is based on the Installation Style Guide and tailored to the specific needs of the project. (4)

Mandatory Relationships	✓	Does the software tool ensure that each **Application Style Guide**
MIS3MR1		belongs to one and only one **Application Development Standards**? (4)
MIS3MR2		is to be based on one and only one **Installation Style Guide**? (4)

Optional Relationships   None

Chapter 20
Miscellaneous

Attributes	✓	Which of the following attributes for each **Application Style Guide** does the software tool support?		
		Name	Description	Validation
MIS3A1		Identifier	Identifier of the guide	Unique
MIS3A2		Description	Description of the guide	Text

Object Representation   None

Quality Criteria   None

Attribute Dependent Tests

Mandatory Relationships   None

Optional Relationships   None

Object Representation   None

Quality Criteria   None

MIS4 Installation Style Guide

Each **Installation Style Guide** has significance as a set of standards about the nature, approach and style of the human factors aspects of computerised systems. The standards should be followed by all projects undertaken within an organisation. (4)

Mandatory Relationships	✓	Does the software tool ensure that each **Installation Style Guide**
MIS4MR1		is to be the basis for one and only one **Application Style Guide**? (4)

325

Testing Criteria for the SSADM
Version 4 Tools Conformance Scheme

Optional Relationships None

Attributes	✓	Which of the following attributes for each **Installation Style Guide** does the software tool support?		
		Name	Description	Validation
MIS4A1		Identifier	Identifier of the guide	Unique
MIS4A2		Description	Description of the guide	Text

Object Representation	✓	Does the software tool ensure that each **Installation Style Guide** has the following object representation?
MIS4OB1		Any textual representation

Quality Criteria None

Attribute Dependent Tests

Mandatory Relationships None

Optional Relationships None

Object Representation None

Quality Criteria None

Chapter 20
Miscellaneous

MIS5 Physical Environment Specification

Each **Physical Environment Specification** has significance as specifying the hardware and software products and services to be supplied, commissioned and made available for implementation. Generally, this will be provided by the vendor. (6)

Mandatory Relationships	✓	Does the software tool ensure that each **Physical Environment Specification**
MIS5MR1		belongs to one and only one **Physical System Specification**? (6)

Optional Relationships None

Attributes	✓	Which of the following attributes for each **Physical Environment Specification** does the software tool support?		
		Name	Description	Validation
MIS5A1		Identifier	ID of specification	Unique
MIS5A2		Description	Description of specification	Text

Object Representation None

Quality Criteria None

Attribute Dependent Tests

Object Representation None

Quality Criteria None

327

Annex A Index of Products and Concepts

The following table lists all the products and concepts in the testing criteria, giving the identifier for each in the questionnaire. Also given is a cross-reference to a chapter in the SSADM Version 4 Reference Manual describing the technique where the entity (product or concept) is created during an SSADM project. This will assist the reader who is familiar with the Reference Manual, but not the grouping of products in the British Standard. The references given are in the format [Module identifier] - [Chapter identifier]. (Where a concept exists for the implementation of the testing criteria only, there is no such cross-reference).

Entity Name	Testing Criteria Reference	Reference Manual Module & Chapter Reference
Access Path	FDF54 (concept)	RA-LDM
Application Development Standards	MIS1	PD-IPD
Application Naming Standards	MIS2	PD-PPS
Application Style Guide	MIS3	F-DD
Attribute Representation	PDD52 (concept)	PD-PDD
Attribute Type	LDM55 (concept)	RA-LDM
Attribute/Data Item Description	LDM1	RA-LDM
Business System Option	BSO51 (concept)	RA-BSO
Business System Options	BSO1	RA-BSO
Candidate Key	RDA52 (concept)	RS-RDA
Capacity Planning Input	TSO1	LS-TSO
Command Structure	DDN1	F-DD
Command Structure Option	DDN57 (concept)	F-DD
Common Process	DFM59 (concept)	RA-DFM
Composite Key	RDA56 (concept)	RS-RDA
Compound Key	RDA55 (concept)	RS-RDA
Condition	LDP54 (concept)	LS-LDPD
Context Diagram	DFM1	RA-DFM
Cost/Benefit Analysis	BSO2	RA-BSO & LS-TSO
Current Services Description	RDF7	RA-SM (Stage 1 product)

Testing Criteria for the SSADM
Version 4 Tools Conformance Scheme

Entity Name	Testing Criteria Reference	Reference Manual Module & Chapter Reference
Data Catalogue	LDM2	RA-LDM
Data Flow	DFM54 (concept)	RA-DFM
Data Flow Diagram - Level 1	DFM2	RA-DFM
Data Flow Diagram - Lower Level	DFM3	RA-DFM
Data Flow Model	DFM4	RA-DFM
Data Store	DFM52 (concept)	RA-DFM
DBMS Data Storage Classification	PED1	PD-PDD
DBMS Performance Classification	PED2	PD-PDD
DFD Process	DFM51 (concept)	RA-DFM
Dialogue	DDN51 (concept)	F-DD
Dialogue Control Table	DDN2	F-DD
Dialogue Element	DDN53 (concept)	F-DD
Dialogue Element Description	DDN61 (concept)	F-DD
Dialogue Element Descriptions	DDN3	F-DD
Dialogue Level Help	DDN4	F-DD
Dialogue Structure	DDN6	F-DD
Dialogue Structure Node	DDN52 (concept)	F-DD
Dialogues	DDN5	F-DD
Document Flow	DFM57 (concept)	RA-DFM
Document Flow Diagram	DFM5	RA-DFM
Domain	LDM54 (concept)	RS-RDA
EAP Node	FDF52 (concept)	RA-LDM
ECD Node	EEM54 (concept)	RS-EEM
Effect Correspondence Diagram	EEM1	RS-EEM
Effect Correspondence	EEM56 (concept)	RS-EEM
Effect	EEM52 (concept)	RS-EEM
Effect Qualifier	EEM55 (concept)	RS-EEM
Elementary Process Description	DFM6	RA-DFM
ELH Node	EEM53 (concept)	RS-EEM
ELH Operation	EEM58 (concept)	RS-EEM
ELH Structure	EEM60 (concept)	RS-EEM
Enquiry Access Path	FDF1	RA-LDM
Enquiry Process Model	LDP1	LS-LDPD
Enquiry Trigger	FDF53 (concept)	RA-LDM
Entity Description	LDM3	RA-LDM
Entity Life History	EEM2	RS-EEM
Entity Representation	PDD51 (concept)	PD-PDD
Entity Role	EEM57 (concept)	RS-EEM

Annex A
Index of Products and Concepts

Entity Name	Testing Criteria Reference	Reference Manual Module & Chapter Reference
Entity Type	LDM51 (concept)	RA-LDM
Event	EEM51 (concept)	RS-EEM
Event/Entity Matrix	EEM3	RS-EEM
Event/Entity Matrix Entry	EEM61 (concept)	RS-EEM
Exclusive Relationship Group	LDM56 (concept)	RA-LDM
External Entity	DFM53 (concept)	RA-DFM
External Entity Description	DFM7	RA-DFM
Feasibility Option	BSO52 (concept)	F-FS
Feasibility Options	BSO3	F-FS
Feasibility Report	BSO6	F-FS
Foreign Key	RDA57 (concept)	RS-RDA
Function	FDF51 (concept)	RS-FD
Function Component Implementation Map	PPS1	PD-PPS
Function Definition	FDF2	RS-FD
Function Definitions (Set)	FDF3	RS-FD
Functional Requirement	RDF51 (concept)	F-RD
Grouped Domain Description	LDM4	RA-LDM
I/O Descriptions	DFM8	RA-DFM
I/O Structure	FDF4	RS-FD
I/O Structure Descriptions	FDF5	RS-FD
I/O Structure Diagram	FDF6	RS-FD
I/O Structure Diagram Node	FDF55 (concept)	RS-FD
I/O Structure Element	FDF56 (concept)	RS-FD
I/O Structures (for all functions)	FDF7	RS-FD
Impact Analysis	BSO4	RA-BSO & LS-TSO
Implementation Of Place Near Logic	PDD57 (concept)	PD-PDD
Installation Style Guide	MIS4	F-DD
Integrity Constraint Representation	PDD55 (concept)	PD-PDD
Logical Data Store/Entity Cross-Reference	DFM9	RA-DFM
Logical Data Store/Entity Cross-Reference Detail	DFM60 (concept)	RA-DFM
Logical Data Structure	LDM6	RA-LDM
Logical Database Process	LDP51 (concept)	LS-LDPD
Logical Database Process Node	LDP52 (concept)	LS-LDPD
Logical Database Process Operation	LDP53 (concept)	LS-LDPD

Entity Name	Testing Criteria Reference	Reference Manual Module & Chapter Reference
Logical Design	PSN2	LS-SM (Stage product)
Logical Grouping of Dialogue Elements Description	DDN60 (concept)	F-DD
Logical Grouping of Dialogue Elements	DDN54 (concept)	F-DD
Logical Key Representation	PDD54 (concept)	PD-PDD
Logical Process Model	LDP2	LS-LDPD
Logical System Specification	PSN3	LS-SM (Module product)
Logical/Physical Data Store Cross-Reference	DFM11	RA-DFM
Logical/Physical Data Store Cross-Reference Detail	DFM61 (concept)	RA-DFM
Mechanism For Retrieval By Key	PDD56 (concept)	PD-PDD
Menu	DDN55 (concept)	F-DD
Menu Structure	DDN7	F-DD
Menu Structure Node	DDN56 (concept)	F-DD
Non-Functional Requirement	RDF52 (concept)	F-RD
Physical Data Design	PDD1	PD-PDD
Physical Design	PDD3	PD-IPD
Physical Design Strategy	PDD2	PD-PDD
Physical Environment Classification	PED3	PD-PDD
Physical Environment Specification	MIS5	PD-IPD (input to Module)
Physical Process Specification	PPS3	PD-SM (Module product)
Physical System Specification	PSN4	PD-SM (Module product)
Pre/Post State Indicator Value	EEM59 (concept)	RS-EEM
Process Data Interface	PPS2	PD-PPS
Process/Entity Matrix	DFM13	RA-DFM
Process/Entity Matrix Entry	DFM62 (concept)	RA-DFM
Processing Specification	PSN1	RS-SM (Module product)
Processing System Classification	PED5	PD-PPS
Prototype Demonstration Objective Document	SPP1	RS-PRO
Prototype Pathway	SPP2	RS-PRO

Annex A
Index of Products and Concepts

Entity Name	Testing Criteria Reference	Reference Manual Module & Chapter Reference
Prototype Pathway Component	SPP51 (concept)	RS-PRO
Prototype Pathway Component Query	SPP52 (concept)	RS-PRO
Prototype Pathway Component Result	SPP53 (concept)	RS-PRO
Prototype Result Log	SPP3	RS-PRO
Prototyping Report	SPP4	RS-PRO
RDA Working Paper	RDA1	RS-RDA
Relation	RDA51 (concept)	RS-RDA
Relationship Description	LDM7	RA-LDM
Relationship End	LDM53 (concept)	RA-LDM
Relationship Representation	PDD53 (concept)	PD-PDD
Relationship Type	LDM52 (concept)	RA-LDM
Report Format	DDN8	RS-PRO
Requirements Catalogue	RDF1	F-RD
Requirements Specification	RDF8	F-RD
Resource Flow	DFM56 (concept)	RA-DFM
Resource Flow Diagram	DFM15	RA-DFM
Resource Store	DFM55 (concept)	RA-DFM
Screen Format	DDN9	RS-PRO
Selected Business System Option	BSO5	RA-BSO
Selected Technical System Option	TSO5	LS-TSO
Service Level Requirement	RDF53 (concept)	F-RD
Simple Key	RDA54 (concept)	RS-RDA
System	DFM58 (concept)	(Scheme only)
System Description	TSO2	LS-TSO
Take-On Requirements Description	RDF2	LS-TSO
Technical Environment Description	TSO3	LS-TSO
Technical System Option	TSO51 (concept)	LS-TSO
Technical System Options	TSO4	LS-TSO
Training Requirements Description	RDF3	LS-TSO
Update Process Model	LDP3	LS-LDPD
User Catalogue	RDF4	F-DD
User Catalogue Entry	RDF54 (concept)	F-DD
User Manual Requirements Description	RDF6	LS-TSO
User Role	DDN58 (concept)	F-DD
User Role/Function Matrix	DDN10	F-DD
User Role/Function Matrix Entry	DDN59 (concept)	F-DD
User Roles	DDN12	F-DD

Bibliography

Information Systems Engineering Library

The Information Systems Engineering Library volumes, published by CCTA, are available from HMSO Books (Dept A), Freepost, Norwich, NR3 1BR, or telephone 071-873 9090, fax 071-873 8200.

The following volume is referenced in this publication:

A Guide to the SSADM Version 4 Tools Conformance Scheme, 1993

ISBN 0 11 330589 3

ISSN 0967 9561.

Appraisal and Evaluation Library

The Appraisal and Evaluation Library volumes, published by CCTA, are available from HMSO Books (Dept A), Freepost, Norwich, NR3 1BR, or telephone 071-873 9090, fax 071-873 8200.

Overview and Procedures, 1990

ISBN 0 11 330534 6

ISSN 0967 957X.

CASE Tools, 1993

ISBN 0 11 330609 1

ISSN 0967 957X.

Other Publications

British Standard BS [nnnnn], Specification for information systems products using SSADM.

The Standard is available from British Standards Institution, Sales Administration, Linford Wood, Milton Keynes, MK14 6LE.

SSADM Version 4 Reference Manual, 1990, is published by NCC Blackwell and is available from The Publications Manager, National Computer Centre Ltd, Oxford Road, Manchester M1 7ED. ISBN 1 85554 004 5.